The Body Is Art

The Body Is Art

✦

A Mentoring Guide for the Business of Massage and Bodywork

Diane Matkowski

iUniverse, Inc.
New York Lincoln Shanghai

The Body Is Art
A Mentoring Guide for the Business of Massage and Bodywork

iUniverse books may be ordered through booksellers or by contacting:

iUniverse
2021 Pine Lake Road, Suite 100
Lincoln, NE 68512
www.iuniverse.com
1-800-Authors (1-800-288-4677)

ISBN: 978-0-595-43477-0 (pbk)
ISBN: 978-0-595-87804-8 (ebk)

Printed in the United States of America

Contents

Acknowledgments

I would like to give special thanks to all Freedom Massage clients, especially our regulars, for your support and inspiration. You have all had a positive impact on my life and have given me a great opportunity to enjoy being human. Freedom Massage would not exist without you, and I give my best wishes to all who have walked through our doors.

Thank you to all past and present Freedom Massage practitioners: you have all taught me so much.

Thank you to all of my mentors who paved the way for the evolution of body-work and massage.

Thank you to my stepmother Sylvia, for your love and support. Love you.

Thank you to my brother Jason. You are a wonderful brother and friend. Love you.

To my accountant and one of my mentors in business, Tony Ivanoski: thank you. Freedom Massage would not have survived without your patience.

Thank you to the center of how things get done: Darla, my bookkeeper.

Thank you to Marc Heppe, Devon Heppe, and Jennifer of DH2 Design Communications for putting together a wonderful cover. You rock! DH2 Design can be reached at www.dh2.com.

Thank you to Frances Reed for the mosaic artwork for the cover. Thank you to Jessica Morris for the photograph for the cover. Freed Mosaics can be viewed at Freedmosaics.com

Thank you, Computer Wiz, Chris Griffin of Custom Tech Solutions, Inc, who recovered this manuscript from my dead laptop! If you have a computer crisis, he is the man.

Thank you to Nikki Gray, Michelle Fallon, Judy Gray, Dana Maxwell, Leslie Strange, Jennifer Stoltenberg, Jessica Stolle, Melinda McBride, Rebecca Hardy, BethAnne Pacera, and Martha Heckel for reading this book before it was completed.

I would like to give special recognition to Martha Heckel. I love you. You are one the most incredible friends around.

Rosemarie Montague, "Lova," my friend and mentor: I love you.

To Amy Bartosiak: thank you for your extra love and support.

Mandy Moore, thanks for the ride, love you.

Thank you Ashley, Kat, Allison, and Jen. Love you.

Thank you to my family, friends, and loved ones, whose quiet contributions will never be forgotten and will be forever appreciated.

Last, but not least, thank you to iUniverse for your generous time and support.

Examples of Tables and Forms

Employee contract

Client information

Client agreement form

Follow-up sheet

Cancellation form

Corporate chair massage agreement

Client tracking

Pay sheet

Preface

I am happy to say I have been in the business of massage therapy for almost ten years. I graduated from the Owens Institute in Delaware. I also studied at the Integrated Institute of Nutrition, the Ohashi Institute, and with Michael Buck, Rick O'Brien, and many other wonderful folks. Before my venture into the world of massage, I acquired an associate's degree in business administration and spent several years in sales. I have built a business, Freedom Massage, from just six clients to nearly two thousand. I have five employees. My interest in developing my own career, as well as the careers of my peers within Freedom Massage, has led me to create a volume on the practicalities and business of massage therapy. My focus is to help answer questions I have heard from many of the new practitioners I have mentored. In this book, I try to give an intimate look at my ideas, some of which I have found might need more focus after the educational process. After witnessing too many good massage practitioners burn out too quickly because of frustrations on the business end of their practice, I recognized a need for a quick-reference guide to support growing practitioners and their businesses.

I wanted to share the knowledge I wish I had found in the beginning of my career. I share practical advice about professionalism, intuition, education and mentoring, bookkeeping, accounting, contracts and other documentation, and so much more. Let my accomplishments and mistakes be a guiding force as you enter into or build your own practice.

Introduction

This is a guide to help you with the business of massage therapy, whether you are new to the field or working to strengthen and expand your practice. I will discuss the finer qualities of the amazing ritual of massage, provide assistance in rejuvenating your business if you are having trouble keeping clients, offer suggestions on how to expand your services, and give you ideas on how to flow with the ups and downs of a practice and enrich your practice's outreach to the community. Just as important, this volume contains guidelines to the more practical aspects of your practice, and it also includes ways to create opportunities for your clients to become more aware of their bodies' needs through routine bodywork.

By my own revelations and experiences from nearly a decade of successful growth in this business, I hope to enhance your journey into bodywork and open your mind to the practicalities and endless possibilities for healing that a massage therapy business can provide. I will share business advice and my views on how to become a better bodyworker. I will offer ideas on how to deal with sometimes challenging decisions that come with managing your massage business.

As massage has grown in popularity and demand, it has become a business. The business world and its complex workings should be considered an asset, full of tools and tips to expand and aid your thoughts, to help understand the actions and motivations in the world, and to learn how to bring your skills to the forefront to reach your personal goals. Self-proclamation and a fresh demonstration of business and integrity will be a guiding light for our art to bring positivism to the world. Business is a powerful creation, and, in its working, there is a huge opportunity to enrich the public's view of bodywork. Business touches all social structures in our country. If we turn our heads away from this world and pretend it does not exist, our art will not exist. Because business is ingrained in our social structure, massage must become a business in order to sustain the people who want to see the practice of and appreciation for massage grow.

Economics and marketing are streaming through everyone on some level. Each of us can use business and its workings to expand our networks of people, ideas, self-worth, and understanding of the world. We, as practitioners, can dwell on the fringes of the business world, but we cannot avoid it altogether. Frankly, why would we want to when so much opportunity dwells within its makeup?

Through sharing our art and working within the defined rules of business and professionalism, more people will seek bodywork as its reputation improves. When a massage practitioner presents the benefits of massage to the layperson in a relatable and understandable way, they can move mountains by bringing a healing touch to a larger sector of the community. Your life as a massage practitioner, when blended with the business world, can help you grow into a stronger person then you might have imagined.

A career in massage can be quite stimulating if some of the finer details of the art are not overlooked. Massage provides clients and practitioners with the ability to become more conscious of human bodies on many levels. You will watch your clients' bodies and lives change through their sessions with you. The body is a castle, an architectural achievement that is both unique and astounding. We all dwell in similar, yet completely different castles, and with each massage, your client experiences different emotions and physical sensations. Every session with your client can be seen as a journey into the unknown. By focusing on your passion for bodywork and recognizing the vast potential—both professionally and personally—in this business, you can truly experience the joys of this art.

I have seen many people in this business come and go, but the two-year limitation or burnout period in massage therapy is, in my opinion, a myth. With the right tools and know-how, such as the ideas presented in this volume, you will be able to endure in this business and achieve longevity on this exciting journey. Unfortunately, some practitioners never discover the joys of the work due to lack of time in the business. They miss becoming a more mature practitioners by skipping many chapters that unfold during their development. In fact, some of the greatest discoveries a massage practitioner can make take months, even years, to grasp, and even then are only accomplished through the dedication of a professional practitioner—both in actions and business practices. In order to receive all bodywork has to offer, it is important to recognize yourself as a professional businessperson and an artist. With this outlook, your career will bloom, as will your self-esteem.

You will have a variety of experiences once you begin doing massage, and I hope to give you insights into some before they occur. These insights are designed to help you prevent some things that I had to learn the hard way, and to help you build confidence in the practice you may have already established. As a mentor, which is a part of my practice that I find particularly important to my personal growth, I recognize the importance of being mentored and listening to the stories and ideas of people who have been practicing bodywork for years. After almost ten years of practicing massage, I have learned much about my own needs and how to serve the needs of my clients. Much of this knowledge has come from time and experience, and from other practitioners who have shared their insights with me, as I hope to do for you. I can see twenty clients a week, have a social life, love my work, and barely break a sweat. My hands are strong, as is my passion for the work.

In order to help you, the practitioner, I will discuss energy maintenance and intuition, which are a large part of being a successful massage practitioner. It takes time to understand your limits and the things you feel but might not see. While it is important to have passion for massage and for helping clients, it is also important to know about the financial side of the bodywork business. For many people entering the massage business, financial instability becomes an issue. I will also go into some detail about expanding your client base and how to prepare to ride the waves of a career that can be unpredictable at times. It takes effort and patience to learn to recognize and ride those waves. Because ups and downs in revenue are a part of this business, it is important not to fight against them; instead, let the waves wash over you and carry you to a more fruitful shore.

I will talk about the details I have learned about new practitioners, through mentoring, and the questions they ask once they begin their career. I hope to help you enhance your strengths and to share my years of experience in a simple way. I hope to add excitement to the work by sharing the details of business and show-ing how they run parallel to all of life's experiences. The profession of bodywork is a fulfilling and enriching experience when the proper steps are taken to enjoy the work. It is my desire to deepen your love for bodywork through my revela-tions.

Life is an amazing journey; make your own rules and abide by them. "We must be the change we wish to see in the world," is one of my favorite quotes by Mahatma Gandhi. It is our responsibility as practitioners to create positive per-ceptions of bodywork and what it will offer to our communities. We all know the saying, "You never get a second chance to make a first impression." With our presence, we can be a doorway to a lifestyle change, and the power of touch will redefine body awareness for each client. As a massage practitioner you have an opportunity to be a part of important changes in your clients' lives.

I am offering you a quantum leap into the world and business of massage ther-apy. I don't ask you to agree with my perceptions, but perhaps you will build from my experiences and philosophies to cultivate a strong and beautiful practice.

1

Philosophies on Building your Foundation

TRANSFORMATIVE QUALITIES OF MASSAGE

Massage is an incredible way to help people relax and grow. Touch was, and remains, a natural instinct. When a mother hugs a child or rubs his knee when he falls, it works like a remedy. Through expanding upon the healing quality of touch, people are delving deeper into its relevance as a means of preventive health care. Some people have moved away from touch, but the art of massage can bring it back to them. Massage has an incredible effect on the human body, and with consistency you will help clients transform their lives.

I have many clients who say massage has changed them on many levels, from feeling better overall, to having more desire to exercise, to having more flexibility, and the list goes on. I, too, have been touched by the transformative effects of massage. My father and stepmother took me to a massage practitioner when I was nineteen, and my first massage was a thought-provoking and interesting experience.

During that first massage experience, I instantly became aware that I had a body—in some weird way, it was truly the first time in a long time that I really realized I had one. Until then, I never took note of how my calves or my forearms felt. I had received gentle touch as a child, but I was unaware I could feel my muscles beneath my skin. I always knew they were there and had seen them on charts, but I had never received therapeutic touch so intense. I never felt blood and oxygen rush into my muscles without moving them, or when I was in a relaxed state. It is a feeling I still adore.

Until then, my body got me around, but I had never seen it as such a complex machine, holding the truth of who I was and my experiences. I felt myself behind layers of skin and muscle. I was suddenly slowed down. I was forced to think

1

about the body surrounding me. I was provoked by the sensation of thumbs deep in my muscles. It was the first step on my never-ending journey to self-discovery. Massage helped get me back to my body and filled me with the desire to experience the essence of touch and being human.

As a teenager, I took my body for granted—and I still do on occasion. Even as an adult, sometimes I am just too busy. At times people indulge in things mindlessly until the effect on their body becomes obvious through exhaustion or pain. After my first massage, I began to awaken and discover that all the answers were inside of me and in the very skin surrounding me. I realized that my actions and what I put into my body had a direct relation to how it/I felt. I began to see my body as a map: a landscape of all my thoughts, experiences, and emotions. My body has literally grown with me from infancy to adulthood and has provided me with the mobility and ability to experience life.

My body is an expression, but it is also the dwelling place of all that I am. I am completely responsible for my actions. My body is my tool and partner in experiencing life. The mind and body are a dynamic team. During my first massage, I experienced the revelation that my body was a vehicle. It is an absolute masterpiece, far beyond anything the hands of man could make. The history of my life was contained in this body, and I slowly began reevaluating everything in my life. Massage was my gateway to self-discovery, and I was blessed to have my father and stepmother bring me to a bodyworker when I was so young.

By combining all of my experiences, listening closely, and having compassion, I would create reliable tools within myself to make good decisions. Bodywork has given me a true understanding of the many benefits, seen and unseen, of receiving self-care modalities. However, I still do not fully understand, nor have I discovered, the many lessons my body holds. The journey we take through touch is never-ending, and it changes—as does the very makeup of our bodies—every day.

We all come from varied backgrounds, which we refer to as good or bad, but everyone has a past. Everyone has lessons to learn and struggles to overcome, no matter how their past looks to the outside world. With so many visual stimuli in today's world, at times it may be difficult to overcome the distractions to see ourselves and to see our own potential more clearly. There are no simple answers for any of us, but we are free to enjoy life's beauties. Bodywork creates a space for reflection and relaxation, a place to unwind from the struggles of the day. It gives us a tool to better understand the world inside of us and helps us adapt to the world around us—not to mention that it feels great and relaxes the body.

Unfortunately, many people disregard the needs of their bodies and are unable to appreciate the physical and emotional benefits of knowing how their bodies feel. The obesity rate across America alone is evidence that the body is being over-looked. So many people are on autopilot, flying through their days. They are often detached from the workings of their inner selves, perhaps even from their emotions, and they have unknowingly abandoned the concept of knowing their bodies. I believe people spend much of their time in their minds, wrapped up in their thoughts, and not enjoying the five senses the body offers. It makes the experience of life so much more gratifying to really feel your body. Sit still and think about all five of your senses. Smell the air, feel your clothing, listen to all the sounds, really see your environment, taste; notice everything around you, and revel in being present with your body.

As the body unwinds and relaxes, it gently whispers the answers. I learn many things each day through working with the human body. Our bodies have been through every experience with us. The body holds the memory of every step and action we have ever taken and the key to everything we have become. It is our means of transportation and is directly related to how we see the world. I realized that by listening to my body, I was learning to understand its needs. I know when I need rest, assistance, comfort, or care. Through my practice, I have realized that ignoring a body and emotions leads to pain and sometimes disease. We must understand our bodies, and massage is one means of fulfilling this exploration. Our body is our three-dimensional image of what lies inside. I once heard some-one say, "It is not just a body, yet we are our bodies." Without a connection to your body, I believe it is difficult to fully appreciate being human and a body-worker. Massage helps us realize the transformative qualities of touch.

PROFESSIONALISM

Professionalism should be the cornerstone of your practice. Within the confines of society, people expect and desire contact with a professional in all aspects of life, from the deli counter to their own office space. Professionalism does not mean just acting properly and politely in a work situation; it is defined by a broader scope of responsibility to your chosen craft. In the art of massage, this is a duty of purity and consciousness. It is about exerting effort, not only to do a ter-rific massage, but also to provide a wonderful experience. For professionalism to reach its full potential, the desire to be a true professional must come from within the practitioner.

I have actively defined how I see a professional massage practitioner. I think it is important to gather the tools necessary to be the professional you want to see more of in society. I have done this by listening to massage mentors, observing my own behavior, noting the behavior of my clients, and using my practice as a classroom. Your massage practice can be a modified version of the classroom we found ourselves in as children. Thankfully, we are finally outside the school setting provided by the education system, and we are free to roam the planet as we choose. As adults, our classroom is filled with the never-ending possibilities of nature, and our potential to succeed as massage professionals is limitless. The beauty of nature's classroom is the freedom to create the life we desire and deserve.

Professionalism is an opportunity to enjoy and excel in our strengths and embrace our lesser strengths. I enjoyed the moments of growth in my practice and continued to move forward, gathering tools on my path. There have been moments where I have said the wrong things or given the wrong pressure while doing a bodywork technique, but these became my learning experiences. We are in a vulnerable state, both as practitioners and as clients. We all learn as we go, but we must remember that as a massage practitioner, it is important to be professional.

The realization that I had, to be the best professional I could and truly take responsibility for my practice, came after a conversation with one of my mentors. We were sitting on a porch in the woods amid beautiful mountains, and he said simply, "If you are going to be a massage practitioner, you need to be the best practitioner you can be, because right now it is what you have decided to do for a living." He told me he attained all the beautiful things in his life by being committed to himself and his profession. No matter what career he had, he practiced it with all his heart. He enjoyed his work, realizing that each job or situation was a step toward a dream he was creating. He went from working on an oil field where people would put rattlesnakes in cars for fun to having a multi-million-dollar home in the mountains—as a second home.

He really gave me a deep understanding of the importance of enjoying myself while trying to be the best at what I am doing in each moment. He said it is important not to get ahead of myself and think too much about the future, but to create what I wanted right now. He firmly believed "being in the now" was the only way to be authentic in what you do, and it was a quality that created the integrity that any good person needed to succeed. He also told me, "You need to decide if you will sink or swim. I don't know about you, but I would rather swim." He helped me realize that I was completely responsible for who I am and where I am in life. I have a responsibility to myself to make good use of my time and to fully enjoy myself in regard to my profession. I was going to swim, and I decided to become one of the best at my chosen craft by being a true professional.

I went from working out of my car doing house calls, to working out of my condo, and now I own a small business on the Main Line, an affluent area outside of Philadelphia, Pennsylvania. My first location is still my space seven years later, but things have changed dramatically. Freedom Massage began with me taking a leap of faith and renting the second floor of a house and transforming it into a little getaway. For the first several months there was a phone on the floor, a massage table, and nothing else. I worked diligently and focused on building the practice and finding practitioners who wanted to work for me.

It seemed like a slow process, but in just two years at my new location, I went from seeing my twenty clients to having a business that serves two or three times that many people, and which now supplies massage for other practitioners. Now Freedom Massage is the only business that occupies an entire commercially zoned home in the area. There is still a phone, but it is no longer on the floor. The house is furnished with a hint of Asian influence and has been transformed into a massage haven. Freedom Massage has a client base of over two thousand wonderful clients. I presently employ five practitioners, and we work as a team to spread the joy of the art. We are a quality, not quantity, facility.

We have the opportunity to help people wake up and feel their bodies. By providing an exceptional massage for our clients—a professional experience that is therapeutic for the body and specific to the person's physical and emotional needs—we can help create an atmosphere that is less stressed and help people to better enjoy their lives. Through exceptional thoughts and bodywork, we can create our dreams. By truly believing in our life's work, we will have a greater impact on the world around us. I believe being a massage professional in the highest regard means refining your abilities and constantly growing as a practitioner and a person.

Much of our lives take place within the boundaries of our profession, and this time spent should be as enjoyable as possible to attain true balance. Many massage practitioners get caught up in the job. We forget we still really are on the outside of corporate America looking in at a tired group of folks. We still need to participate to survive and grow, but we do not need to follow the same rules or give our lives away in the same way. Part of being an excellent professional is enjoying what you do. When the experience of building a practice is used wisely, creating professionalism can be a gateway to the self and enhance your understanding of your character. Massage can be used to help you meet people where they are and build the relationships in all aspects of your life. Be active in creating your practice; treat it as if it were a piece of clay and create the sculpture you desire. Reflect on how you would like it to look and how your practice can help you work to your fullest potential. Bear in mind that you are able to be everything you wish to be. Nothing can hold you back but your own fear. Believe in your intuition. Cultivate your practice by knowing yourself.

Massage practitioners have the potential to enhance self-discovery, opening the doors to better enable self-realization. We may play an integral part in the awakening of a body and renewal of a soul. Our massage can be a treat. Our massage table can be a mini-vacation from life's struggles, inviting in the joy of life. The possibilities are endless in your journey as a bodyworker.

ENERGY MAINTENANCE

Each practitioner must determine the actual amount of physical, emotional, and financial energy needed to flourish in their business. We must acknowledge and understand our own thresholds. You cannot push past your limits, or you may create disharmony in your body. Honor and respect your threshold, or you, the practitioner, will quickly become burned out. When our emotional and physical aspects are out of balance, one aspect may overshadow the whole person. If you are struggling financially, it will also be a distraction and wear you down physically and emotionally. I refer to keeping this balance as energy maintenance. Each encounter with a client is a physical and emotional experience: if equal attention is not given to your physical and emotional state, balance will not be maintained. Physical, emotional, and financial energy must be used wisely. For you to excel as a practitioner, your body must maintain energy to do its work. To a degree, these energies are scarce resources and can only offer so much each day. Support your strength and enjoy your work! In the beginning of my career, I did seven or eight massages a day, Monday through Saturday, and then I rested on Sunday. This proved to be a great physical demand on my body. Meanwhile, I took no time to evaluate my emotional well-being, my place in the world, or my personal goals. We may power through our massages physically, give to the clients before ourselves, and fail to acknowledge the emotions that arise for us as practitioners. My vision was set on the *quantity* of massages I was doing, only to find myself feeling alone and disconnected from the intimate relationships in my life. Not only was I disconnected from my personal life, but at this point in my career I was working alone and was thus cut off from professional interactions with fellow practitioners as well. My first several months in the business were very difficult, because I constantly pushed myself beyond my threshold. The result was a week or two where I could barely do a massage without struggling emotionally before, during, or after a session. In the beginning of my career, as I booked myself beyond my ability to keep balanced, an art became work.

On the other hand, when my emotional energy was overcharged, I would have weeks where I wanted to solve the emotional problems of the world. I would make myself vulnerable to clients and carry their woes and the weight of their concerns. I went through the weeks thinking of everyone else. I did not take time to go for a walk or have personal time to regroup, until, suddenly, my sore thumbs and hands would remind me that I forgot form and style, due to diving too far into the inner world of my clients. I was working too much on everyone else and forgot about myself.

Massage is a wonderful career, but in order to succeed, it must also be financially rewarding. Neglecting your body or emotions will leave you weak, frustrated, and exhausted. It is just as important to realize times of financial hardship can cause your physical and emotional state to become even more stressed. Being unable to pay bills or do things you enjoy will leave practitioners tense and unfocused. It is a very fine line to keep an emotional, physical, and financial balance, and it takes time and dedication to find your own comfort zone. When you first start out, it is safe to play with your energy limits and push yourself. But once you have discovered them, they must be maintained. When you honor your energy balance, it will show itself through your body's wellness, your mind's joyful desire to work, and feelings of prosperity.

The mind plays a powerful role in maintaining energy in bodywork. Oftentimes it is good to take a few minutes to prepare the mind the night before sessions, awakening the body's craving to heal itself and help heal others. Epsom salt baths, making sure you get massaged, and a healthy diet are imperative for the physical being. In the same regard, meditation, reflection, healthy and supportive relationships, honesty, and taking responsibility for ourselves are important for our emotional well-being. Also, being financially prepared will give you a comfort, helping you to feel safe and secure. The body and mind must both be rejuvenated to provide a gateway to optimal health.

Physical Energy

We must first understand our own physical energy to help others do the same and to excel as practitioners. There is no end to studying your physical limits, and they might change regularly. It is a lifelong journey, which only ends when the body is laid to rest. Climate, food intake, and many other events keep the physical energy in a constant state of change. Truly moving with your limits will always lead you in the right direction. As a practitioner, it is necessary to honor and respect the moment by being true to how much energy you require to keep purity in your actions. Take note of your own physical state. Remain true to yourself if your body feels tired or pushed too hard. Learn how to manage your work in correspondence to your personal physical abilities. Again, I also invite you to look at what you are putting in your body. Find foods to help your body be healthy. See food as the fuel to help keep your physical state strong.

Once you begin understanding your physical limits, you will be better able to evaluate your clients. You will hear and feel stress in their voices; you will see it in their eyes, their walk, their faces, and all of their physical features. Practitioners have been studying physical traits for hundreds of years and documenting their findings. By studying your own features and expressions and observing others, you will begin to recognize and understand levels of energy maintenance. In turn, you will be able to gauge how much energy is appropriate for each client. By paying attention to your physical limits and recognizing theirs, you will begin to do a dance while performing bodywork sessions.

Listening to how much your body says to give will allow you to always have enough energy. Thankfully, this gift, cultivated through the practice of bodywork, will seep into every aspect of your life. Remember, some people will take and take until you are exhausted, so learn how to have boundaries. Be honest when you are giving of yourself and recognize how much the client needs and makes use of your efforts. It is important to realize that some of your clients will not want to hear your opinions and are happy as they are in life. Your clients' happiness is your main concern, and if people are happy as they are, we should be happy for them.

There are people who will remain in pain even after many sessions. It may take time for them to learn how to relax and take care of themselves. There are some who will not let go of their pain. Your work will feel easy when you are with people who want to get well. Clients who want physical miracles without effort on their own part will drain your energy. Healing through massage takes two people to be successful, so it is your work plus the client's ability to let go that begins the healing process. If you do not use your physical energy wisely, you will find that an hour is not enough time to accomplish all your clients' desires. When you finish your last client, your energy will be gone. Keep boundaries and know your limits.

Evaluate clients and listen, but do not get caught up in their distractions and exhaust yourself trying to fix them. People may rattle off ten things they want resolved in an hour. Remain calm and address the issues you can in a session. Be clear with your client and explain what you can realistically accomplish with the time at hand. Realize that you are simply on a path with clients and there is no known destination. It is a long journey, and you will not completely relieve a client of stress accumulated over many years with one session—or sometimes even in several sessions.

It is not your job to miraculously heal people, but there is a chance you might experience their choice to be healed. Not until the client resolves the issues creating stress and disease in the body will those symptoms diminish. Understanding this is crucial to physical maintenance. Be patient and do not try to do too much too quickly. Help them realize that their pain has been building over time and is one of the body's calls for attention. Practitioners cannot unwind years of action in one or two sessions. Perhaps there will be a huge amount of relief, but without consistency and change, the pain will return. You will exhaust yourself trying to heal every person in every session. To practice true energy maintenance, the giver must enjoy the art and dance to the rhythm that the client's body is playing.

Over the years, I have been able to create harmony in my schedule. I have been very precise in my planning, yet I have left room for surprises and even additional clients. It has taken some time, but if you understand physical energy maintenance early on, you will not take as long to create such a schedule. Find clients whom you enjoy working with and with whom you feel you are making progress. If you are working with the right people, even clients with a lot of physical issues will be a pleasure.

I have a client who is a very successful businessman, and he has very little stress in his life. He is in his fifties and has learned to accept life and its challenges. When he comes to my office each week, he seldom complains about any aches or pains. He does not talk much, and he sinks deep into the table. His attitude makes my job easy. He allows me to practice my art. He is game for whatever I have in my toolbox. I have to exert very little energy for his massage, and it is a joyful experience working with him. If there is a specific issue, his body accepts my work very quickly. Usually by the end of the session, any disharmony is resolved. His body appears to be better every week, and together we are maintaining a healthy state. Our physical energies work very well together. I can approximate how much energy I will need for his session and plan my other clients accordingly.

My client after him does a lot of physical activity and has a very stressful job. His head is extended forward, his shoulders are hunched, and his back is raised and tense. His body is tight, and there is very little movement, as if he is frozen in emotional and physical stress. My client really wants to unwind, and I am supporting this process. Since he has been coming weekly for massages, his head and shoulders are receding, and his back is softening. Sometimes I do very deep massage on him, and we are awakening his body. Every week the session is different based on his needs. I use slightly more energy in a session of this nature, so I schedule him as my last client of the day.

You will find that some clients may sleep through sessions. It may be the only true rest their body receives. Even in a deep state of rest, your client still receives the many benefits of your work, and you will receive the benefits of performing a relaxing massage. Allow the client to fall into a deep state of relaxation, feel the rhythm of their sleep, and conserve your own energy. Our massage should follow the client's tone.

Help your client reclaim stillness; unconsciously the comfort of our care will have positive effects beyond what we could even imagine. Take good care of the client, but realize this time could be a time for you to slow down as well. Follow the rhythm of your client's body and understand how to maintain your physical energy.

Emotional Energy

Bodywork is based on and surrounded by life's struggles and joys. You will be working closely with people, and it is easy to get emotional when you are in such an intimate setting. Be aware of your emotional energy and do not give too much away. Clients may be in a very vulnerable state: when there is dysfunction or disease, emotions will reveal themselves. I suggest choosing not to give too many personalized perceptions; instead, lend an ear and be present. I prefer not to give advice to my clients. Do not be consumed by the emotions of others, because it will cloud your vision and your ability to help them heal.

There will be clients who want to give you a lot of personal information. You will be working with so many different personalities and types of people. You will hear some interesting things and witness the human being on many different levels. You will need to learn how to blend and enjoy a lot of different people. Be a strong force in their lives and remain firm in your decision to have boundaries. Throughout your sessions, your clients may express feelings, and you must carefully watch your own. Do not take things personally or become too involved.

Our job is to do bodywork and support people, but remember, we are not trained psychotherapists. Hear your clients, but do not take on their struggle. Sometimes it is better not to have all the answers; rather, let your clients figure things out on their own.

I try to see the good side of things for clients, so I can be a positive force. In my experience, anything else usually turns out to be more emotionally draining. I would like to reiterate that we are not psychotherapists and that it is okay not to be. Life is already full of emotionally draining and provoking events without adding more at your workplace. Remember, you only see clients once a week, maybe less, which is not very much time to draw conclusions. Imagine two rooms: you have a room and so does your client. During a session, the rooms are side by side, and there is an invisible dividing wall. Both of you see each other clearly, but it is important to stand firmly in your room. And if you do travel into their space, remember your anchor. Keep your room neat and clean for sessions so you are clear on what is your stuff.

Furthermore, a client's session is certainly not a time for you to discuss your problems. Keep your personal problems out of the massage room. If clients ask how you are, keep your response simple and remember it is their time of relaxation. You are in a service business, so it is important to remain positive. We all have many things to experience and understand about life. Each journey is important and equally filled with lessons to understand. Keep in mind your own journey and allow others to experiences theirs.

There will be clients who come to socialize and talk throughout their session. Again, keep things simple and allow the relationship to grow with time. Many of my clients know a bit about my personal life, but it has taken years of consistent sessions and careful consideration. I have learned that I need to save energy to deal with my own emotions, to process the emotions of those around me, and to understand how I feel about the interactions throughout my day. Leave some room for your own emotional healing, family, friends, and life. Stay focused during client interactions and use your emotional energy wisely.

I had a client who would enter my office with a huge frown or sad face for *every* visit. Every day was a bad day. After the sessions, she still seemed sluggish and depressed. It seemed her life was a struggle. Her days were full of drama and chaos. She would talk session after session about everything wrong in her life. She was emotionally exhausted and also exhausting to me. I saw her for quite some time with no change. It was hard to keep my spirits high when visit after visit she remained stuck. Her list of ailments continued to grow as she went to therapists, doctors, and numerous places to find people to tell her what was wrong.

I felt that I had embraced the reasons she had come to my practice, and I reflected on our relationship. My bodywork and approaches did not seem to break through, time after time. She was quick to complain, but she did not make changes. She asked for stretches and exercises, but she did not take the time or effort to do them. I had to make a decision to maintain my own emotional energy. Finally, I recommended her to another bodyworker.

Some clients teach us about letting go. We are not meant to work long-term with every client we meet. We should not keep troublesome clients for fear of losing a source of income. As in day-to-day living, you should end a relationship that continues to cause you grief. It is hard, but if you find yourself feeling drained after every session, you should really consider having the client see someone else.

I also have a rule: what is said in the massage room stays in the massage room. I never share client information under any circumstances. Sometimes it is tempting because I massage entire families who are excited to tell me news. Every time I hear it from a different family member, I treat it as though it's the first time.

Everyone has agreed on a time schedule. Every person has twenty-four hours in a day, and I have grown to cherish every moment. My emotional energy maintenance is crucial to my well-being. Straying from the effort of taking care of oneself creates disease and disharmony. Save time and energy for yourself and your loved ones. Every day is another chance to love, grow, and become our true selves—a person who is no longer overshadowed by the illusions of perceptions. We are not practitioners to resolve our clients' emotional struggles, but to help healing grow within them. Standing back and observing is sometimes more powerful than having a lot to say.

Financial Energy

As a massage business owner, I have watched other practitioners come and go. I believe some have overlooked the financial burden of building their own business or building a client base in someone else's. Once you have established yourself as a practitioner, you have freedom. Prior to this, you must plan your finances wisely.

I took about a $30,000 pay cut *before expenses* my first year in bodywork. Do not fool yourself into thinking that there will be twenty clients dying to see you every week as soon as you complete your massage program. It is a possibility, but I believe it is an unlikely one. If you are feeling a financial burden at the start of your career, it will be very difficult to build a practice. I suggest planning for a period of a financial drought. Realize that you will have very little income in the beginning stages of your practice. It is possible that you will need a bit of time to adjust to this new career, and if you are not massaging, it is likely you won't be getting paid.

When I started my journey in massage, I did not realize that it would take nearly six months to build a solid client base. For anyone coming into the massage therapy business, I suggest having ample savings or keeping a job with guaranteed income on the side. You will only be able to massage so many people per week, so plan wisely. You will need to figure out exactly how much income you need and how many massages you can consistently do per week. Figure out whether you plan to work with a company, on your own, or both. It will take time to build a faithful clientele no matter what you decide. It will take time to achieve your goals, so be patient, persistent, and compassionate with yourself.

You will need sheets, a table, oils, accounting materials, and many more supplies. Shop wisely. There are great deals on leftover tables or tables with small tears in the lining. If you call Oakworks and ask them about these tables, they will be happy to sell you one. Keep in mind that if you are self-employed or an independent contractor, you should expect to pay about thirty percent of your wages to the government. There will be overhead costs and expenses to be deducted from the post-tax amount. If you choose to become an employee and see your first paycheck, you might think you make less per hour. However, it is important to note that you will be taxed fifteen percent less than someone who is self-employed. If you go on an interview, be sure to ask what practitioners average in tips. You might find that you can make about the same money as you would on your own, and you will have less responsibility because you would be working for someone else.

Before my career change into massage, I made sure I had a stable home. I bought a condo prior to my career change, because it can be difficult to get a loan when you are self-employed. I made sure I had a good car and other things I thought were important to my own comfort. If you are making a career change into massage, you might want to consider creating stability in these areas. Balancing emotional and physical energy is very important to attain financial wellness in the career of massage. You will need to continue massaging and earning money week after week. It is important to know your limits so that you can create the money you need to live peacefully. It is also important to have financial stability so that you are able to find peace physically and emotionally. The possibilities are endless as long as you have all of the basics covered.

ABCs of Sharpening Intuition

One of the most important parts of bodywork is intuition, or trusting that you will know exactly what to do during sessions. Intuition can also be defined as believing in what you feel and what to do to accomplish goals, setting your hands free to enjoy the landscape of the human body, and allowing yourself to travel outside of sequence and to let the body before you direct your session. I believe part of intuition is realizing that having faith in your talent is one of your most valuable assets.

I was blessed with a mother who realized that we had school classes for mathematics and language arts but not one for our sixth sense, or intuition. At a young age, I recall telling her that I thought my friend Connie would call, and about a half-hour later the phone rang—and Connie was on the line! My mother would become excited at such events. She always believed we could see more without our eyes and that we realized more with our gut feelings. Intuition has become a word some see as intimidating or "New Age-y," but it is a gift inside all of us. I believe that it is our cosmic connection to the unseen and unspoken. It is a feeling beyond our emotions and, in some cases, even our imagination. It is a tool we can use to help us make decisions in bodywork and in life.

My mother played games with me as a child, which I now realize were helping to sharpen my intuitive tools. She would do things like put her hand behind her back and ask me to guess what number she was holding up. As my skills were honed, I became more aware of the feelings I would have when I guessed right and wrong. I also remember one instance where she was sitting on the couch scolding me, and I must have seemed like I was looking into outer space. She asked me what I was doing, and I told her she had a color around her body. Without hesitation, she went upstairs and got her book on auras. She looked up the color and saw what it meant. She congratulated me on my intuitive abilities, and then she resumed scolding me.

There have been times when I have been lost while driving, and my gut told me to turn right, and suddenly I was back on track. I have met people and known them for just a few moments, yet some part of me knew that we would be dear friends. All of these events are intuitive qualities shining through. I am not asking anyone to start searching for auras or to do psychic readings. In fact, I am not even validating such practices. I will, however, make suggestions on ways to become in better harmony with everything going on around you. Being in rhythm with your surroundings can help you be more in tune with clients. Intuition will help you keep clients and help them grow, and it will help you make productive decisions in your own life. This section is the most difficult for me to express, because intuition is so abstract.

Sometimes it is the people that we are closest to who unknowingly dim some of our intuitive qualities. One of my closest friend's mother laughed at her as a child when she said that she wanted to be an actress. Therefore, the seed of uncertainty about her abilities was planted. At age thirty-four, she still remembers that moment vividly. She had an idea—rather, a dream—and shared it with someone she trusted, and that person let her down. It is a story she has told me more than once. Now, I watch her struggle with trusting the ideas and ideals she has for her own life. She is one of the most brilliant people I know, but she still struggles with that moment, and I believe moments like this can hinder our innate intuitive qualities. I think we all have similar moments that we need to make peace with in order to excel.

By getting to the root of self-doubt, we can strengthen our gift of intuition. I believe it is our responsibility to unmask illusions and fears planted in our minds by negative life experiences, setting our minds free to reach our fullest potential. Though everyone has the potential to master their own intuitive skills, it is a character trait demonstrated—or even realized—by very few people. For intuition to be sharp, you must understand your relationship with yourself and acknowledge your of areas of lesser talents and distrusts.

It is not a myth or a special talent, but our given right and attainable reality to be in tune with the rhythms of the universe. We have the power to choose wisely through the quiet whisper of our unseen intellect, and we can exude the power of our intuition. It is important to choose words wisely and to let go of words that may have hindered your self-confidence. We can help our clients' intuitive qualities bloom or fade. It will be very important to understand your thoughts and how to process them as you grow as a bodyworker.

Here are some simple clues on how I believe you can awaken your intuitive qualities:

Twelve Clues

1. Intuition equals instinct

Watching nature is a great tool for sharpening intuition. As a squirrel glides through the sky as it jumps from branch to branch, it does not hesitate. Is a squirrel's lack of hesitation intuition or instinct? I believe it is both. Because we are humans, we have choices, an idea that adds a whole new element to the word "instinct." Believe in yourself and what you feel. Every moment and every experience is important and relevant. It is important to be as present as possible to gather the information we need to truly embrace our experiences and allow our intuitive and instinctive qualities to surface.

When I first started learning how to play the drums, a mentor told me, "There is no messing up. Just keep playing, and people will not even notice." Learn the importance of not being critical of our experiences; instead, embrace them and "keep on keeping on." Following instinct is our nature, but it has been overshadowed by social construct and conformity. By rediscovering intuition, we are getting back to our instinct and true human nature. Re-learning to trust our instinct and quiet the chatter of our mind can help us decipher what thoughts are relevant. Remember, "There is no messing up." Even when you think you are off track, you can gather the tools you need to strengthen your instinct by focusing on your present situation. As you continue on your journey, your vision will become even clearer.

Follow your instincts while building your client base. I found that by building my practice, I was essentially creating my life. One of the first steps is being aware of yourself, having complete honesty about your conclusions, and learning to follow your instincts. Follow your truth, your instinct, and your intuition without fear.

2. Pay attention to every detail

Every moment is loaded with details. As my mother said, "Thousands of thoughts pass through my mind, but I choose which ones I hear and evaluate." The answers to life are as ever-changing as nature. If you can learn to listen to your feelings, pay attention to what you hear, and dismiss what is not relevant, then you will learn to follow intuition. Another mentor said, "It is not our thoughts that make us who we are, but what we choose to do with the thoughts." Thoughts may seem random, but if you take note of what you are feeling and thinking, you might find the answers you are looking for to discover yourself. Try experiencing life as if it is all being presented for you to learn from and enjoy. You are the thinker of your thoughts, not the thoughts themselves. Your mind guides your reactions and your thoughts. Your brain is yours. You are capable of making good choices and can choose to feel how you wish about life. By paying attention to all of the activity in your mind, you will be in balance with the joys life has to offer you.

One of my many mentors taught me to look at my life at the end of each day as if it were a movie. This is a way for me to examine my thoughts and feelings. I pretend I am in a theater watching my day, and even my thoughts are being played over the speakers for everyone to hear. By "watching" my day, I can check in with myself and evaluate how I truly feel about my actions and thoughts—realizing, of course, that tomorrow there will be room for improvement. I remember that I am human. I also realize that every day makes me stronger if I allow it to. Within my body and thoughts, I want there to be a genuine desire to be kind to myself.

Life has ups and downs, moments of chaos and confusion, and times of love and passion—and all are gifts. We think millions of thoughts every day. It is not important for anyone to know them all, but it is important for each of us to understand our thoughts and to realize their power. Our thoughts help us enjoy life and discover the boundless beauty of living. The more you become aware of your own thoughts and greet them with honesty, the better you will become as a bodyworker. Create positive thoughts and enjoy discovering your intuition more and more everyday.

3. Physical similarities

A great gateway to deepen intuitive qualities is by looking at the characteristics of the human body. I took an excellent class at the Ohashi Institute in Manhattan on Oriental diagnosis. This form of diagnosis believes physical traits show us more than we might have imagined. There are many books on this topic such as *Reading the Body* by Ohashi, *Bodymind* by Ken Dychtwald, and *Amazing Face Reading* by Mac Fulfer, JD.

The book *Bodymind* describes thousands of cases about areas of the body that represent similar feelings in people. For example, studies showed people with emotional releases from the chest area during bodywork sessions shared feelings of neglect and abandonment. I discovered this book because I attended a class in Gettysburg, Pennsylvania, where I received bodywork and began crying like a baby. The teacher of the class referred me to Dychtwald's book. I found that the feelings I experienced were consistent with the thousands of others in his studies pertaining to emotional releases in that area of the body.

Ohashi's book, *Reading the Body*, provides information about the entire body and some of its smaller details. For instance, he believes the human ear can tell us a lot about a person's history. Of course, in his classes he is very clear that the entire body must be understood, and understanding this art is a never-ending process. I believe becoming aware of these concepts and drawing upon your own insights is a great tool for dealing with people. It is an awesome way to begin paying attention to the human body and opening your intuition.

There are also face-reading books, which will further direct your attention to even more subtle details, such as the shape of the forehead. Does it protrude at the top or the bottom? Is it flat? It is a limitless study that you can use in the grocery store, with family, and with clients. The human body has been studied for a very long time. My personal observations have shown me that the body is a three-dimensional view of the emotions and who we are as a person. Body reading, face reading, analyzing the body's shape, and other forms of studying the body can be a lifelong learning experience, and the world is your classroom.

Once you know the basics, you can unveil different truths every day. Utilizing body reading, if done correctly, keeps your mind open to the entire body, but it also brings intrigue to the smaller details. Through repetitive thoughts and behaviors, I believe we have created the very structure in which we dwell, the human body. This human body also contains emotional behaviors and patterns passed on through the generations. It has taken many years of observation for body reading to become a tool available for bodyworkers. For me, it has taken years of interest and observation to create my own ideas on the logic of reading the body.

People often remind you of someone else because they have the same qualities. There is a consistency in the mannerisms and looks of certain groups. There are countless jokes told about different characteristics, and many of us laugh because they are undeniable. Everyone recognizes how he or she feels from receiving a friendly smile, but there is so much more behind our face and body. Sometimes appearances can say a lot about people because of what feelings they provoke inside of you. People share similar physical characteristics that can give us clues to their emotional state. In my own personal observations, I have noted that many people with similar physical traits have things in common beyond their physical appearances.

Take special note of the similar physical characteristics between people. The commonalities may not just be in their appearance but also in their emotional approach to life. These signs become more obvious—and intuition is developed—when we are open to the possibility that we are all the same; we just have different expressions of our truths. Through physical similarities, you may see more than you previously realized.

4. Awareness

My father taught me to be aware of my surroundings. He wanted me to wipe the crumbs, and I mean every crumb, off the countertop when I was done eating, and he wanted me to carefully clean the kitchen sink. These seemed like silly, obsessive tasks to me at the time, but I now realize he was teaching me to pay attention to the details. Being mindful as I performed these tasks has carried over into my interactions with people.

I watch the way people stand, walk, and talk. I pay attention to how I feel around others. Do I feel nervous or comfortable? Do I feel safe? Some of my own issues will have an effect on how I feel around people, but it takes both of our energies to create these feelings. The more I am aware of my own feelings, the more I can pinpoint which feelings are mine and which are the other person's. When I am aware of how I feel, I am more able to feel others. When I feel nervous around someone and I look closely at their body language, I may see that it is the person before me who is nervous, and I am simply reflecting or reacting to their emotions. When we tune in to our own awareness, we feel much more intuitively. Being aware better suits us to give our clients the massage of a lifetime.

5. Awareness II: universal truth

The nature girl inside of me feels the power of the earth. It is alive and brings life to everyone who walks on its soil. The earth creates the very oxygen we breathe, yields the food we eat, and has blessed us with a classroom beyond measure. Sometimes the beauty and power of nature is overlooked. It is often treated as just a background. Though nature is not merely a background, but where and how we live. We are suddenly made aware of the magnitude of nature's powers when we hear about disasters such as hurricane or tornado.

For intuitive qualities to bloom and excel, there must be a connection with nature because it gives us life. Everyone needs to find their own connection in their own way. Sadly, this is missing from some people's lives, and it is an integral part of how we survive. I believe many people don't get outside enough. Instead, they go from the inside of their houses to the inside of their cars to the inside their workplaces. Unfortunately, they probably get about thirty minutes of fresh air per day. We could not exist without nature; we are only an aspect of nature, and I believe it could, and would, survive without us.

I spent two months in the mountains of Maine, and I was struck by the beauty of nature and the teachings the earth brought to my ears. Nature impressed me with its vastness. It was the first time I spent so much time alone and outside. In a way, nature has been my greatest teacher; it is in complete balance and harmony. I sat on mountaintops, watched different animals and plants, and looked down at the ocean. It was a perfect painting in motion, and it was all there for my eyes to enjoy.

So many people get caught up in their lives and overlook the many blessings right in front of them. Nature helps us to better be in tune with the values and truths that are important. Someone once said to me, "When you can measure the sky with a ruler, then you know something." Nature helps put the grandeur of life in perspective. The beauty of the changes of the seasons, the deer, the trees, the people: there are so many gifts nature brings to our eyes.

In nature lies a world run by instinct and intuition, a world of mammals, reptiles, insects, and greenery living in harmony with their surroundings, simply trying to survive. A rock will change shape as it sits in a river, but it may take years, reminding me to be patient. The silence of a summer evening brings an orchestra of crickets to put me to sleep. Studying nature will open your heart and mind to a reality bigger than a life focused on day-to-day activities. It will help you deepen your belief in the power of intuition and help you feel a force bigger than yourself, giving you comfort.

Nature is the force that spins the planet on its axis, pushing us all through time and daily living. We can allow its majestic power to move us, or we can get lost in the daily grind. Watching the innocent, yet fearless, beauty of nature may enhance qualities in you, which will help enhance the role of intuition in your bodywork.

6. Be thankful

Good things happen to good people, and even bad things happen to good people, but both can be used to create strength. Seeing the beauty of your work and giving thanks for every client is essential for deepening your intuitive qualities. To share power and do good work, your intentions must be genuine. Your vision cannot be clouded with doubt or judgment. Relish the gift of every client, and avoid getting into a rut. If you do, remember how lucky you are to be making a positive difference in peoples' lives. Everyone is happy to see you, and they feel wonderful after having received your work.

Being a massage practitioner is a gift. You are in a sublime atmosphere, creating positive energy all day. Being in a good massage business gives you freedom. I probably get as much satisfaction out of a session as my client does because I realize that I am actually getting paid to create good feelings as my life's profession.

Being in a state of thankfulness allows our intuitive qualities to surface and resurface on a profound level every day. If you clench your fist, nothing can fall into it. If your palm is open and facing upward, it can be filled. The same is true of your state of mind. If we are not at peace and open, our intuitive qualities will remain stagnant. See your sessions as opportunities, not as a job, and remember to be thankful for each and every one of your clients.

7. Rest, rest, rest

Rest is essential for living a healthy lifestyle and for a clear, crisp mind. I often ask fellow practitioners, "When was the last time you had a massage?" Many times they cannot even remember. Even massage practitioners get lost in their daily lives, leaving their intuitive qualities dulled. I make sure I spend time alone resting and regaining my strength.

In my case, this means lying still or sitting in front of my fireplace looking at a fire; it does not mean plopping in front of the television. Our minds are still active as we watch and listen to the words coming from the television, and that puts our body in a much different space than quiet and rest. Some people believe it is good to sit in front of the television because it is mindless. This might be true, but your body is still affected by what it sees on the screen.

Real rest comes from quiet and giving the mind a chance to unwind. You may find that your mind will go a million places before it realizes that it needs to rest. The mind gets caught up in what our five senses collect during the day. Sometimes we are not only dealing with our own thoughts but also with the feelings and concepts we pick up through our interactions. The human experience is truly beyond words and beyond explanation, but resting and regaining strength to better embrace the experience is crucial. True rest helps us stay in a state of real life by sitting quietly and getting in touch with who we really are outside the ideals of the world around us.

Exercise is a wonderful thing. However, if the body is already in a state of stress, sometimes working out is not the best answer. The body can only be pushed so far before it will rebel. At one point, I was doing eight massages a day after being at the gym for two hours. I was awake at 5:00 AM, lifting heavy weights and doing cardio. My body was carrying more weight than it ever had. It had no time to rest, making it difficult to process food and emotions. I began blowing up like a balloon and felt like I was ready to burst. I was unable to make good decisions on what I ate, and I was constantly in a fog.

Now I do light exercise on busy days, if I formally exercise at all. I finally realized that a long day of massage is exercise, and there is no need to push my body past its limits. I make sure to eat wholesome foods and get enough rest, which is just as important as working out.

I go for walks with my dog, in the morning and in the evening. Her innocence always calms me, as does her excitement to run all over and smell every object popping out of the ground. Every day she enters the outdoors in wonder, smelling the changes, and is excited to see the folks on our trail. I have found a way to get exercise without pushing my body too hard.

Of course, on slower days, I might push myself further, but I have the energy to spare. Everyone should gauge the amount of energy they are putting out and realize that the body needs to be balanced with real rest. Recent studies show that inflammation is the body's first response to discomfort and might be the beginning of disease. Inflammation stems from stress, poor diet, overwork, and inadequate rest.

To be in tune with our intuition, we must be in tune with ourselves. We can achieve this by allowing our bodies and minds time to have real rest. It is in the moments of rest that you will feel your intuition begin to surface. You will get past the random and rapid thoughts of the day, and hear the truth about yourself. You might even begin to see your own endless potential and vision for a healthy, happy, and productive future.

I believe that silence, like nature, is another great teacher. If we cannot be alone with ourselves, how can we expect the world to want to be around us? No matter what your situation is, finding the time to spend in quiet solitude is possible and crucial. At first, it might seem strange and a bit uncomfortable, even scary and boring, but stick with it and be true to the feelings you experience. Rest and unfold the intuitive nature dwelling within your body. It will become stronger, and you will be well rested to give fantastic bodywork sessions.

8. Honesty

There are so many different views on how to live life. Be honest with what you feel, and cultivate a deeper relationship with yourself every day. We all feel honesty on different levels and approach it differently, but honesty and taking responsibility for who we are is crucial. It will deepen all understanding and give a bodyworker the ability to be authentic and genuine. You clients will feel the difference.

9. Getting full of life, not of food

Selling cars (yes, selling cars!) for three years was one of the most difficult, yet awakening, experiences of my life. I worked at a "one-price dealership," where there was no commission; instead, we were rewarded for volume. I had countless people come in with very good values and ideas. I had to learn how to interact with every type of person, because everyone is different and at different stages of life. These stages have become educational and fascinating to me as I experience my own life.

I remember one day I was sitting in the dealership with a couple, and when I took their driver's licenses, I was amazed to learn that they were in their forties. At a glance, I would have guessed they were just thirty. I asked them how they kept their youthful glow. They said, quite simply, "You are what you eat." They taught me that your appearance is a reflection of what you put in your body. The husband giggled and said, "If you eat a Big Mac, you are a Big Mac."

Since that time, I have become intrigued not only with the outside of the body but also with the inside. My latest educational experience was at the Integrated Institute of Nutrition, in Manhattan, where I learned the latest ideas on nutrition. Like many New Age concepts, the IIN's ideals go back to the basics of eating well, reminding us all to eat less processed food and get back the richness of whole foods. When you eat processed sugars and other foods in excess, it takes an incredible amount of energy for your body to maintain balance and break them down. Therefore, your mind is left cloudy and your intuition foggy. Also, when you fill yourself with too much food, your body works overtime to find balance, and your mind gets lost in the process.

It is important to find food that your body can easily process and that gives it nutrients. It is important to consume food which will provide the body energy. For your mind to be clear, the food you put in your body must be of good substance.

As a practitioner, it is your responsibility to find out what it means to eat well. It takes real rest and reflection to be in tune with what the body needs. I encourage you to do some research and begin to truly understand your body's nutritional needs.

Pay attention to how different foods and drinks make your body and mind feel. If you put diesel fuel in a car that runs on unleaded gas, your vehicle will not run properly. It is the same with the human body. You might not reach your full potential if you put improper foods in your body. The best meals are the ones you prepare yourself with whole, rich foods that your body will know and love. If the body is properly fueled, the mind and body will work in harmony. In this state of being, your intuitive qualities will more readily appear—and shine.

10. Do not invade

I have interviewed countless practitioners, and, thankfully, part of the interview is a bodywork session. My staff takes turns with this part of the interview process. During one interview, the practitioner giving me bodywork entered the room and announced that he was going to give me energy work. I took a deep breath and held my tongue, realizing that my role was to allow the practitioner the freedom to show me his art.

However, if I was a new client, which is how the practitioner should treat me on an interview, such an announcement would be unacceptable and invasive. Some people do not know what energy work is, and they might not want a stranger performing something called "energy work" on their bodies. I, too, would also prefer that someone ask permission to perform this type of work. There is enough of an energy exchange that occurs during a session with a focused intention; I had no idea what I was going to receive, nor did I know too much about this gentleman. I felt a bit overwhelmed by his announcement and found it very difficult to relax.

Similarly, giving intuitive advice without permission is also invasion. I have spoken out of turn, and the result was confusing to my client. Usually when we invade, we are not prepared to provide the support a person needs. We are more compassionate when we give thought and respect to our clients. We are better equipped to help with their issues or answer their questions when we move slowly and respect boundaries. We hold open a door for a client with a smile, instead of pushing them through hastily. It is not our job to save the world, but to be prepared and wait for an opportunity to help.

If we are lucky enough to feel things at the right time and have the right interactions with a client, our intuition will be in harmony with our client's healing process. Our egos must be left at the door, and we need to remember that we are in a service industry. Intuition is powerful, but do not allow it to be overpowering. I usually wait to be asked questions, because this is when the client is most ready to hear what I might have to say. If my feelings are overwhelming and strong, or if I have the energy to support uncertain outcomes, I will ask permission to provide input.

When I first started doing massage, the lines of what constituted invasion were blurry. I remember a time outside the massage room when I put my hands on a younger woman's back, and all I could think of was her mother. Never having met her mother, and not really knowing the woman well, these thoughts were a bit confusing. In my ignorance, I blurted out, "Tell me about your mother." The woman immediately gave me a bone-chilling look. She angrily asked me why I had said that, and then she began crying. She told me that her mother was dying of cancer.

I had invaded her emotional space by inviting myself in and making her feel emotions she was not ready to share. I also had nothing to offer her on the level she needed in those moments, because I was not prepared to support her in her pain. Needless to say, I learned to be careful with how I share my intuitive hints.

It is important to listen and move slowly. By moving too quickly, you may cause a client to slam a door. Instead, be cautious: if you are getting a strong feeling, ask your client if it is okay to share what you are sensing. The pull should be undeniably strong to bring forth even the question of sharing your intuitive listening with a new client, unless a session is set up to be an intuitive interaction with words.

Realize, to a degree, that sessions are about surrendering to the clients' time schedules for healing. Some clients will only want to keep your work physical, and they will not want to receive your input, but this does not mean emotional changes are not occurring. We are not the judges and juries on our clients' progress or lives.

It is important to remain positive and give support to your client. It is also important not to be like a robber, sneaking in and taking what is not yours. The clients have already made themselves vulnerable by shedding their clothing and allowing you to touch them. Be considerate and cautious with your intentions. In time, you will realize that there are people whose energy you might not wish to ignite too intensely.

Once the line of sharing intuition is crossed, the dynamics of your relationship with the client might change. It will take adjustment and practice to handle such a dynamic. Be kind and patient with yourself and your client. Sometimes even when people ask, they might not be ready to hear your perception, so make sure you are ready for the result of your input.

Also, it is okay to keep things to yourself. This, too, is part of being intuitive. If you do choose to share, present things in such a way that positive changes can be made and negativities can be overcome. Be honest with what you feel, but do so in a gentle way. It may take practice, but do not become discouraged or fearful.

Let your good intentions guide what happens in the sessions. However, I can almost guarantee that not asking permission before giving input will negatively affect your relationship. We must mature as practitioners to understand how to deal with different situations and become comfortable with ourselves. I have been massaging some of my clients for years, and I am noticing that some of my sessions are getting more intense. I too am learning everyday and consistently make adjustments to my boundaries. It is important to always keep in mind that your client will be at their most vulnerable state while they are lying on your table, and all of our interactions must remain respectful, authentic, and professional.

11. Distracting symptoms

Do not let symptoms distract your intuition. Behind every symptom is a cause, which is what we are trying to unravel. The problems manifest through symptoms. Do not be overcome by the symptom itself. An excellent bodyworker must understand that the goal is for the client to get to the source of their pain.

One of my teachers shared the story of a woman who came in for a session. The woman complained of having a terrible headache, and she looked exhausted. She seemed a bit out of sorts and only complained of a sore neck. The teacher said that he felt the problem went deeper, but he honored her space and did not push her. In a later session, the truth finally came out: days before the previous session, the woman had lost her baby. She was wracked with profound weeping throughout the session, and the neck pain subsided. At such times, it is important to hold your space and be patient.

Remember, as practitioners, we have no idea what happens before the client arrives. We only see the symptoms and may not know the cause. Be mindful of what your clients share, but always remember that the cause is a mystery, maybe even to the clients themselves. Allow clients to go at their own pace, and do not waste energy trying to speed up their pace on their unique journeys. Working too hard to fix things will make a practitioner tight. You do not need to fix every person in an hour. Trust what you feel beyond the symptoms you see.

12. Practice

You should not share your intuition unless you are invited, although it should still be cultivated. I now practice my intuitive skills with my fellow practitioners. It has become like a game. I have made practicing fun and not weird or, for lack of a better term, too New Age. I will often describe the inside of someone's home or their parent's home, but only after I am given permission. A simple exercise, one I shared earlier, is to have someone put a number behind his or her back and guess what it is. Another is for you to hold a stone and focus all of your energy into it. Give it to a friend, have them place it in a hand behind his or her back, and choose which hand is holding the stone. This will help you go with your gut and realize how it feels when you select the right number or the right hand.

Mastermind is a great board game for sharpening intuition. This is a game in which your opponent places colored pegs behind a plastic hood, and you get ten chances to guess what colors they picked. Pay close attention to the emotions involved in collecting client information. Learn to recognize how you feel when you make the correct choice. These simple exercises will improve your innate ability to be intuitive. It will also help you to be better in touch with what the client needs, not only by what is said, but also by what you feel.

Have Fun and Trust Your Intuition

Massage drenches the body, quenching its thirst for touch. To provide the best possible massage, the practitioner must surrender to it. The massage itself, not the practitioner, must be the leader. This means completely trusting in your accumulated knowledge of technique and anatomy, and freeing yourself of doubt.

If the client is a boat, and the shore a healed body, the practitioner is the sails. The wind is the intuition to which both the boat and the sails must succumb for healthful living. Intuition, like wind, is not seen but felt. The difference between an average practitioner and an excellent practitioner is the ability to yield to intuition.

The intuition holds the key to success. The sails have been well stitched by the hands of education and practice, and they are the way to harness that wind. It takes time for practitioners—and clients—to develop trust in the wind, but they must let go and allow the wind to blow their sails out in full gale force. The first time that confidence guides the ship into port, and a person's health has been improved, then the energy will flow at a new, fuller strength from the practitioner's hands. Both practitioner and client will reap bountiful healing benefits from this newfound strength. It takes trial and error to understand intuition, but if you are patient, the life rewards are a wonderful asset to your growth. The people who need your work the most will be with you through some of the stormiest seas in their life's journey. Somewhere in their psyche, your clients have surrendered to you, trusted in you, and accepted that you have the ability to take them to their safe harbor.

Every client and every session is like a new celebration for the freedom of expressing your art. Your clients chose you as their practitioner, as their sails. Whatever they receive from you will have a lasting effect, and it will fulfill some basic need within them. The outcome was already unconsciously agreed upon at some level. Once the massage session begins, the outcome your client will receive is, on some level, out of your control. Accept the outcome, and realize that it is merely a lesson for you both. Massage is about being in the moment and realizing that all outcomes are perfect, no matter what course helps you arrive there.

Each encounter with a client offers you an opportunity to embrace and understand the guiding force of intuition that you will learn to depend upon in your practice. This guiding force needs attention, care, and listening to produce a healthy, happy practice. Intuition is a source that comes from within, and it will become the center of your being as you embrace the joy of treating people who truly need your help.

Remember that the gift of massage is not just a healing practice that you offer to another person: it is also a gratifying profession, abundant in blessings, that will give you daily fulfillment as you grow and build confidence. Each interaction will assist you in your own development and help you to better live, love, learn, and share in the healing energy that is your center as a practitioner.

Life is a story, and you are the writer, with many people participating in your script. They will play their parts, and the only responsibility you have is to write your own part. Who will you be? What will you do with this opportunity? I hope you will succeed as a bodyworker.

2

Presentation and Fundamentals Made Simple

ATTIRE

Keep your clothing simple. You should be comfortable but clean and presentable. You want your clients to stay focused on the massage, not unconsciously or consciously judging you. Opt for clothing that is universally known in the professional world as "business casual." Aspiring to a more athletic look is also fine because of the nature of massage—it is about the body and keeping it fit, after all.

Keep your look consistent: I wear khakis or nice gym pants and my logo shirt. Most of my clients have never seen me in anything else. Familiarity is good for the client. Create a comfortable space, not just around the massage table, but also around you. People make themselves very vulnerable by removing their clothing and lying down on your massage table. Consider your attire ceremonial clothing that you picked especially for massage.

Wear quality clothing. You can go to the outlets or any local bargain place and get quality clothing that will fit any budget. Many people who get massaged regularly know quality. This is a simple way to give a client affirmation that he or she is in the right place. It is important to look successful and clean. Through a professional appearance, practitioners can begin validating a client's decision to work with them before the massage even begins.

WINE AND CHEESE/QUINOA AND KALE TREATMENT

Make every massage a special event. One of my sales managers described the service I should provide as an upscale "wine and cheese experience". Offer high-quality service every time. Other practitioners may be presenting peanut butter and jelly sandwiches with soymilk, but you will be serving wine and cheese. Of course, for the food-conscious, you would serve quinoa and kale on china.

Share your passion for providing quality bodywork. It should shine through your skin, beam from your smile, and radiate from your stance. You have received massage from other passionate bodyworkers and understand its many enriching benefits. Remember, it is good to know how different techniques feel on your own body before you perform them on others. Receiving bodywork regularly will give you an opportunity to share your clients' excitement. Listen and act with genuine enthusiasm. I challenge you to listen more than you speak. You are on a stage, and each session is your chance to use the spotlight wisely.

Become a great practitioner and allow the art of massage to flow. Resurrect the idea that touch can heal the body. Remember, massage could help stop disease before it starts. Massage is preventive care, and all the client needs to do is lie back and enjoy your touch, allowing the body to heal itself.

Many people experience a factory-style massage instead of a one-on-one experience. Many massage establishments are concerned with quantity, not quality, because many of the people running the businesses do not practice massage themselves. Even if you are busy, set up your schedule so that you can make subtle efforts to enhance the experience for your client. We have the opportunity to work on the body, to reawaken the masterpiece beneath our hands. The body is an amazing vehicle, and with the power of touch, you will change lives. Enhance the integrity of the lost art of massage, and redefine professionalism.

Feel the massage with your heart. As practitioners, we should be sincere in expressing our desire to accommodate a client's healing needs. Recognize that every person on the planet is on a magnificent journey. Clients give you an opportunity to partake in their journeys for a short time, or perhaps on a longer trail as a professional relationship develops over time. Always serve wine and cheese—or quinoa and kale on a china plate. Massage is your livelihood: excel and be the best.

TIME

Always arrive at least twenty minutes before your client arrives. Clients come to you to relax. They do not need to see you come barreling in before their relaxation time. If you are doing a house call, don't be late: be early—but not too early. Arrive five minutes before your scheduled time every time. People love when they can set their watch by your arrival. I would arrive early for house calls and sit at the end of the street until five minutes before my massage.

Begin your sessions on time and end on time. If you run over with clients, they will begin to expect it. Honor yourself and your time. If you do five sixty-minute sessions in a day and go ten minutes over with each client, then you have almost done an extra massage. Trust in your work and your ability to give relief in the time scheduled. If you are going over an hour, ask the client if they would like an hour and a half. Keep the exchange balanced and get paid for your time. It will help you conserve energy and help you survive as a practitioner.

During house calls, I suggest keeping the "Hi, how are you?" conversation going as you set up your table. Learn how to unpack your table quickly and smoothly. Clients like the show of your expertise even when you are setting up for a massage. They appreciate the timely setup and breakdown of a table. I was always in and out of homes in sixty-five minutes to ensure that I was being paid for my time. Under no circumstances did I stay for social interactions after my massage. It is important to keep business businesslike. If you cross lines and the relationship becomes a more social relationship, versus business, you lose some respect provided by the boundaries of business. I had a client ask me if I wanted to stay for dinner. I was starving, it was late, and I liked the family. I enjoyed the meal and their company. After the evening I stayed for dinner, they seemed to expect I would stay session after session to follow. I felt guilty when I declined and they seemed a bit disappointed. It added unnecessary situations to a good business relationship. I suggest keeping business relationships purely business.

OVERANALYZING

There is good and bad energy in all of us. Feed the good energy so it can grow and overcome the bad. Realize that the universe and all of its energy is bigger than your comprehension. You do not know the true history of your client's entire life. You have not walked in his or her shoes. The only thing you know is that you are witnessing the product of a lifetime of choices. Even if you see a client every week for five years, it is still only hours in comparison to a lifetime. Realize that the client's history is carried in his or her body. Encourage the client to take responsibility, but do not try to explain the unexplainable.

Try not to focus solely on what the client is saying. There are many levels to every session. If you quickly pull out a single piece from a house of cards, it will crumble. Overwhelming a client with too much information may be confusing and might actually slow down the healing process. When the client comes to his or her own conclusions, it will have a powerful effect. Do not have too many expectations for your client's healing process; allow the client to go at his or her own pace.

There are many integral parts to the human structure, and there may be many causes of the symptoms. If you put too much focus on healing a symptom and overlook the cause, the pain may never be dissolved. For example, if a client has lower back trouble and you focus only on the lower back, the neck might be overlooked. In some cases, it is a tight neck causing lower back pain. The neck might remain tight until the client vocalizes hurt from an experience years ago or from an accident they did not mention.

For clients to even begin to understand their bodies, they must first realize that the body is a collection of a lifetime of experiences. Also, to realize their body in its entirety instead of in sections or focusing on specific areas. People come to this revelation on many different levels. It is our job to leave the doorway open for this exploration by helping clients understand their whole bodies. Allow your clients the freedom to discover their bodies on their own.

Remain supportive and help them discover themselves. Your clients are the only ones who truly know what is right for them. If you move too quickly in any direction, the body may be unable to unwind in its most harmonious way. Take your time with clients.

KEEP IT SIMPLE

I believe that another important part of each session is an element of simplicity. A family friend, who handcrafts unique wooden flutes, is of Native American descent, which is very clear from his expressions and appearance. He commands attention and seems to attract people looking for answers. He is the man with the pipe who looks like he lives in a tepee, and he is a guru of sorts.

This man was strolling around at a New Age event, and he came across a woman who was some form of a psychic. She was burning white sage at her booth. As my friend approached the table, she perked up. She asked him if he was Native American, and he replied with a simple yes. She went on to tell him about the powers of sage and how it takes her to another place, and she finds herself floating over the earth. She went on and on about sage. My friend was confused by so much information, so many perceptions; he had trouble keeping up.

She asked, "Native man, how do you feel about sage?"

He replied, "It smells good."

The simplicity of truth and authenticity brings purity to the art of bodywork. Keep it simple, and meet people where they are with a smile.

ALLOW YOUR MASSAGE TIME TO GROW

Learning how to become a massage practitioner takes time, and your studies should continue after school and in every session. Being an excellent practitioner means using your daily experiences to grow. Remember, you will never know all the answers. In fact, some may say you will never know anything. Growth as a bodyworker takes special care and time. I think of it as "the weed or rose" effect. Do I want to be a weed or a rose?

Twelve years ago, on one of my several excursions to spend some time alone in the outdoors, I thought of this concept. I realized that for a rose to grow, it must be placed in a spot with perfect sunlight and must receive just the right amount of water. Loving people who made the effort to help them grow were responsible for planting most of the roses growing in the United States. They had patience from the time they planted the seed until the first bloom. If you want weeds, you can find them growing anywhere. They grow quickly and do not need attention. I want a field of roses. I am willing to wait for the beauty to rise up from the soil.

I realize that every event of my life, no matter how uncomfortable, brought me right here, to this page, able to type my experience. I would not change one moment or rush past one experience to be left with the weeds. Building authentic confidence as a bodyworker takes time, trial and error, honesty, and perseverance.

BE CONFIDENT, NOT COCKY

We have an abundance of information available about many types of bodywork. Sadly, some bodyworkers may start to believe that their way is the only way. If we focus on our desire to help clients in the way we think is best, other healing options may be overlooked. By getting too caught up in one viewpoint, we miss the bigger picture. As Ralph Waldo Emerson states, "What a man does ... What has he to do with hope or fear? In himself is might. Let him regard no good as solid but that which is in his nature, and which must grow out of him as long as he exists." So if we are busy talking about all the good we have done, then we are no longer doing good or creating: we are just standing around and talking. In other words, we are simply pronouncing good, not actively participating in doing good. In order to flourish as a bodyworker I believe it is best to be willing to constantly grow and have it be our nature.

Practitioners who make proclamations about their work and believe they have achieved greatness are likely to become complacent and miss opportunities to grow. Your clients will heal when their bodies are ready, and being cocky will only slow down the process. The client deserves the gratification of discovering the causes of the pain. If we think we have achieved greatness, then we become solid, and we miss the ever-changing flow of the human body. There are countless energies, techniques, and emotions, none of which can be captured through one modality. It is also important to realize other modalities may also benefit your client. Our combined professional efforts can change the nation and perhaps even contribute to the progress of humanity on a physical, spiritual, and emotional level.

AVOID RUTS

My interpretation of something a mentor said goes something like, "If a deer continues to walk down the same path over and over, it will make a trail. If it keeps walking down the same trail over and over, it will begin to make a rut. In time, the rut will become deeper and deeper, and the deer will not be able to see anything but the path."

With this way of thinking, we will never develop our intuitive qualities or reach our full bodywork potential. Keep trying new things. Even if you cannot afford another class, make your table face a new direction or buy new candles, but keep yourself interested and grow as a bodyworker. If you are working with the same clients every week, realize that every day is a new day, and their bodies are forever changing. Allow yourself to enter every session with a fresh perspective. Regular clients are one of your greatest gifts. Treat them as such and avoid ruts.

SHARE, DON'T PREACH

Speak to your clients in a language they will understand. Meet them on their terms, and use dialogue they can easily interpret. Do not talk above your clients. Understand *their* terminology of bodywork. Naming all of the muscles can be distracting and confusing if the client does not know anatomy. Sometimes too much information is enough to cause tightness in muscles. Having too many answers may give clients reason to believe that they are in pain and have little control. Too much information can give power to the symptoms of a cause yet to be discovered.

Help clients overcome pain, and state the positive. Be conscious of your clients' characters, and uphold their desires, but do not enable them to stay in pain. Be genuine in your interactions. Remember there is more that you do not know, compared to what you do know, about your client.

If words are spoken out of turn, they can be detrimental instead of beneficial. Another thing I thought of on one of my adventures was, *words know no time or distance, so their echoes may be heard forever.* It is important to be selective with the thoughts we share with our clients. We are responsible for what we say and do and for our own life's outcome, and in the massage room, to a degree, the effect our words have on clients is our responsibility.

When I was young, my dad told me olives were fish eyes as a joke, and for months I believed him. It was said in fun and intended to be completely harmless, but I believed it until I mentioned it to a friend, and she mentioned it to my entire third grade class. Needless to say, the name "Fish Eyes" stuck for a few years. People will remember what you say even long after you may have forgotten. It is impossible to know how your words will affect another person, so choose them wisely.

Bodywork demands integrity and practice. I believe there are a lot of people with good intentions, but they are missing the authentic piece of communication with clients. Share what you feel, but do not preach your perceptions.

LISTENING

I believe my biggest asset is my ability to listen to clients. My ability to adapt and enjoy many types of personalities is also valuable, because I realize that there is definitely something to learn from everyone. As a mentor to new practitioners, I watch them talk more than they listen. It is as if they feel they need to prove something, and oftentimes they miss a client's potential to spell out the issue they came to resolve.

Overlooking the client's need to talk hinders a comfort that is found only by someone truly being heard. Using technical terms and having overwhelming energy will cause people to retreat, or give them an excuse to leave. In fact, if you are not careful with your word choices, you may add to the list of all the ailments and symptoms keeping people from true healing. I challenge my practitioners to talk as little as possible and listen more. This is a key component in being a true professional. Truly listening enhances one's ability to receive, and in bodywork, you must receive to give the art.

Listening to your client entails being truly present and having complete focus on the importance of what they are saying. Remember, we are in a service business. Many times people pass by and ask "How are you?" but do not wait for the answer. Questions have become gestures, and the power of listening is left behind. It takes careful listening and persistence to fully express professionalism and the benefits of bodywork, but you will have better results if you truly believe in yourself and your profession.

BE AN INDIVIDUAL

I heard a young girl from Africa proclaim, "You are an individual. Be an individual. Do not blend in. Blend out." It really got me thinking about the excitement of my work and how, for all these years, I have allowed myself freedom of expression with my work. It is exciting to be in a field where you can create your own masterpieces session after session.

Be true to who you are, and take pride in the style of massage you bring to clients. Move forward in the direction that best suits your talent. Do not be afraid to be a unique artist. For instance, the artist Jackson Pollack created unique art for his time. Pollack's art is valuable, and his originals are very expensive. His paint splatters may have seemed like a waste of time to his peers, but his passion lives on. I had the pleasure of seeing one of his paintings in a museum and realized they were not just paint splatters at all. His art is filled with passion and depth. It is truly art. This is true of many artists and writers who are now famous. They merely expressed their passion and followed their art. Now, their pieces are considered masterpieces to some. I wonder if Pollack ever imagined I would be looking at his art today in the Philadelphia Art Museum, or if he simply was in the moment and embracing his passion? By the looks of it, and how he broke the boundaries for art of his time, I would say he was motivated by a desire to express himself with art ruled by passion.

Take what you learned from your past experiences, and refine it into an expression of who you are now. Trust and believe in your strengths, allowing them to shine, creating a more solid professional life. You should also know your inadequacies. Honor them, but do not waste energy wishing they were not there, because *your strengths need you.* Share who you are as a practitioner with your hands, and embrace the gift of giving.

SEASONS OF CLIENTS

Like massage practitioners, clients have cycles and seasons, too. People are busy with their lives. If they get out of their massage schedules, do not take it personally or panic, because worrying will only make matters worse. Sometimes appointments slip people's minds, and you will need to call to confirm their appointments regularly. Cancellations may seem to come all at one time, but they are part of the cycle of life. It does not make you an inadequate practitioner. Remember, sometimes you need rest and might not have the judgment to give it to yourself, so the world around you will create a time for it.

Life also brings tragedies such as layoffs, deaths, divorces, and illnesses, which lead to a change in our clients' lives. It is important to check in with people when things of this nature occur and simply let them know your care and concern. I have heard clients complain about their previous practitioners' disregard for such events. A client told me he felt overlooked when he missed a few appointments due to a death in his family. He was a weekly client and was surprised at the lack of response from his previous practitioner. He never went back.

Sometimes life just gets the best of people, and they are happy to hear that you notice they have not been around. These simple acts of kindness have helped my business grow. Clients are supporting me, and I believe it is important to show them my appreciation. Breathe, remain calm, and stay positive, and prosperity will come your way.

CONTINUING EDUCATION CLASSES

I have watched many eager massage practitioners enter the realm of massage therapy with great enthusiasm. They get out of school and fill their schedules with various continuing education classes. I call these folks "class crunchers." They finish their base modality—Swedish massage, Shiatsu, or Thai yoga bodywork—and they take class after class within weeks of one another. I believe this can be counterproductive to the art. Each modality is a different way to create a solid base; they are building blocks. You should allow each class and each modality to resonate before you hastily move on to the next.

Experience through using a modality will show you your strengths and dislikes. Through this exploration, you will be more able to choose continuing education classes. It takes time and a greater understanding of the body to be able to freely express a modality you have learned. Only experience can teach you a truer understanding of each art. I believe it takes at least a year or two of hands-on experience to even begin understanding the skills you are taught while studying a modality. Furthermore, every practice is a lifelong practice. Successful bodyworkers remain students throughout their careers because every session is different from the last.

To be an excellent giver, it is important to receive bodywork in the new modality so you know how it feels, and so you will understand the healing potential of the style on your own body. This will help you share your modality with your clients on a deeper level, because you will be witness to the changes it has brought forth in your own body. I think the beauty of bodywork is that its never-ending possibilities could take a lifetime of learning.

Your greatest lessons will be using your base modality, and different expressions of it, in each session from beginning to end. Hands-on experience and interactions with clients are priceless ways to grow as a bodyworker. Be patient and learn your art; it will make you better in the long run. Enthusiasm is a crucial part of starting out in any pursuit, but for an artist, perfecting your talents takes time and practice. Ultimately, it cultivates your character and style.

Every style of bodywork was created through free expression, beginning with a solid base or belief. Most of the modalities we study today developed through the sweat and experience of a single practitioner who, having dug down into a source of passion, took the time to learn and reinvented someone else's interpretation of the body's needs to create a new art form.

You might find that rushing the process will put you in classes that you later realize you did not want to take. It may also distract from understanding your base modality in the deepest way possible, which I believe is important to achieve success.

When I told one of my teachers I was writing this book, he said, "Take time," and it has. The time has been worthwhile for the experience I have gained. The same teacher reminded me that it took thirty-five years for him to expand his school. Life gives us the great gift of time, so don't expect to know every nuance of every modality right as you come out of the gate—and never stop pursuing a deeper understanding of what this healing art has to offer.

Keep your personal style development in mind as you begin exploring bodywork. Do not act quickly and spend money on classes before you have a strong foundation in your base modality and understand what the new modality will add to your strengths. Save some money for building your practice instead. Remember, your sessions are learning experiences. As your client base and professional outlook grow, choose classes to enhance your strengths and make the most of your education.

3

Massage Techniques and Tips/ Tricks of the Trade

GET OUT OF THE BOX

I have heard countless times how difficult it is to find a good massage practitioner. People have told me that there are "real" massages and "fluff" massages. Many of my clients travel for business, and they come home to Freedom Massage with stories of their other massage experiences. I hear things like, "The lady just covered me in oil. I'm not sure what else she did," or "The massage felt so robotic." Some practitioners seem to go through the motions and never truly dive into their work. They don't push themselves outside of the sequences that they learned in school.

Create a style for each client, each session, and be true to your art. The first step to an incredible massage is listening to your intuition and setting your hands free. Be passionate. Do not think too much about what you're going to do to clients; give yourself the freedom to allow the session to be new with every client and create itself moment to moment.

Over time, you will see that some of your creations are similar to many techniques being taught by other people. Just as the core of some religions seem to be similar, your study of different modalities will show you that they have similar cores. If you have been carefully experimenting with your work, you might have self-taught some of the techniques already available. Many people ask me if I've studied Lomi Lomi because of the way I use my forearms. I've never taken a Lomi Lomi class, so I guess you could say I taught myself some parts of the technique.

Massage is so much more enjoyable when you make new discoveries and venture outside of the box. Let go of your perceptions and allow the texture of your client's body to lead you. Allow yourself to use an improvised form of bodywork.

We express a silent language and create our rhythms through our touch. Sound and rhythm provoke different positive reactions in our bodies on a subconscious level. Improvisation involves listening to that rhythm; there is no set tone, only the steady beat of life. Improvisation is the way to unleash your full potential as a practitioner. It gives you the freedom to do what you feel is necessary to help your client relax and heal during every session.

ALL IS FAIR

When I was a child, my cousins and I would tickle each other's feet and scratch each other's backs. We would form lines and take turns doing light touch forms of bodywork. I have practiced these techniques of relaxation for years.

In my career, when I finished a massage session, sometimes my instinct was to gently scratch over the sheets. Now, I have clients who request back-scratching. I have seen my Wednesday night client at 6:00 PM for eight years. We have tried all kinds of techniques to get her to relax. Finally, we realized that back-scratching was her favorite part of the massage. In her case, it is what relaxes her most.

During some of my sessions with this client, I spend about thirty minutes scratching her back. We realized that it is truly the way to get her into her deepest state of relaxation. I believe some of the greatest healing happens in these times of peak relaxation. Doing deep work on her has a negative effect, and she does not get into the state where her body can truly let go of stress.

One evening, while I was scratching my client's back, she recalled stretching over her mother's lap in front of the television as her mother scratched her to sleep. If you talk to most folks, they have memories of childhood and the caring touch of family or peers. Caring touch adds an element of comfort to your massage.

Don't forget to rub people's toes. I like having my fingertips squeezed. Gently brush over the client's face at the end of a massage. Match a vigorous technique with a soothing one to balance things out. The list is endless—do not overlook touch that you have enjoyed yourself. So I say, "All is fair." Some clients love back-scratching, and some like feathering strokes. I believe these techniques are the closest to the touch we can recall from childhood. Light touch techniques can bring clients into one of the deepest states of relaxation. Find out what your clients enjoy, and help them relax by doing it.

EXTREMITIES

Spend time on the hands, head, face, and feet unless the client asks you to do otherwise. Our hands are our main means of touching and feeling. The sensation of a good hand massage is worth your time during sessions. It is a great way to truly relax someone.

Clients also enjoy having their scalps massaged. Most people love to get their hair cut because of having their hair shampooed! They like sitting back and having their head rubbed under warm water. You can give them the same joy during your massage session. Remember, there are muscles on the head waiting for your attention.

So many clients have told me that no one ever massaged their faces. Spend time on the jaw, the sinuses, and the forehead; these are great relaxation and healing techniques.

Finally, don't forget the feet. I often wonder how many miles my clients have walked on their feet. A car with a hundred thousand miles starts to look a little rough, and yet we have the human foot carrying our weight throughout our lives. If clients agree to it, foot massage with depth and intention will get you far. Try not to overlook these areas, and give them special care.

MORE SKIN ON SKIN

One of my mentors said, "The more skin on skin, the better," and this concept has been my guiding light. I took these words very literally, and every time I had a body in front of me, I tried to discover new ways to get more skin on skin. Do not hesitate to get as much of your body as possible working for you, within reason. I have found that many parts of the human hand, forearms, and elbows will fit magically on a client's body. Be daring and find your own ways to make new discoveries through bodywork sessions with each client.

I have been a massage practitioner for ten years, and I still discover new ways to get more skin on skin and find alternative ways to tackle issues. For example, when I massage the hamstring, I use one hand on the hamstring and massage the foot with my other hand. I try to cover as much of the client's body as I can with each stroke and consistently try to use both hands and forearms, or an elbow and a hand. I may have my elbow in the lower back and gently massage a shoulder with my other hand. I have come up with many creative ways to make sure the client feels engulfed by my presence in each session. Hesitating will be a "buzz kill" for clients. Have fun trying different techniques to get *more skin on skin.*

Seek out Thai yoga bodywork, or take a class at the Ohashi Institute in Manhattan. Ohashi also has sister locations in Maryland, New Jersey, Vermont, and Illinois. As an internationally known bodyworker, Ohashi and his instructors carry a wealth of knowledge. His practice, called *Ohashiastu,* will show you how durable the human body is.

Ohashi believes that, with positive intention, it is difficult to actually hurt anyone. His practice will give you a large variety of ways to make the most of your body while working on someone else's. I do most of my work on the table, and I've incorporated some of these techniques on the table or have done them on the mat once the massage is over and the client is dressed. The results are great. Ohashi's method incorporates ancient techniques that I've found to be very helpful. Make sure you find a teacher who is authentic. Clients will be impressed by your diligence, your variety of techniques, and your dedication to getting the job done.

WORK FROM YOUR CENTER

The sky's energy comes down to the body and is met by the forces of energy coming up from the earth. The pelvic area is where the two collide, and it is known as the body's source of energy in many forms of bodywork. Your hips should be a point of focus and intention. They are your anchor and your strongest point of expression in bodywork. The power you will find in your hips goes beyond any strength your limbs can produce. Your hips should be used like a flashlight shining toward whatever area of the body you are working on.

Through this commitment, your work will become more like a dance. Your touch will be more powerful and stable. Clients will notice a difference in your touch in comparison to someone working from their shoulders. The other parts of your body are merely expressions of the power coming from your hips. Your legs are like the roots of a tree grounding your work and helping to direct the power of your hips. Your arms are recipients of the power; they can freely dance.

If you are truly working from your hips, and the table in front of you was moved away, you would fall over. If you are working on a mat, then you will be leaning your hips forward with the motions of your arms. All of your energy should be leaning into the client. Working from your hips will make your work deeper with very little effort. If you find your hands shaking when you work, reposition yourself and move in from your hips. It is like a dance, not a challenge.

I am well-known in my community for deep tissue massage. I thought my strength came from my curiosity and pursuit of bodybuilding. I did not totally surrender to the concept that my hips were my source of power until I lost about thirty-five pounds and went from a size twelve to a size six. Once my weight settled, it was as if I was working in a new body. I was a bit intimidated by deep work. I wanted to be the strong woman I had been and go deep into the muscles.

I struggled, working with my upper body to compensate for what I thought I had lost. My muscles were shaking in sessions when I was trying to do the same work I had always done. My upper back and wrists began to ache. I wondered if I would be able to do the deep work as a smaller woman. Finally, I heard the voices of my bodywork teachers in my head, reminding me to work from my hips, to dance over the body, to use as little energy as possible, and to enjoy myself.

I lowered my table a bit and began leaning into clients with my hips even more than before, and the result was incredible. I actually had to use less pressure on people who could not get enough in the past. When I began using the power of my hips on my clients, my shaking disappeared. Try it for yourself: pick up a dumbbell and lift it over your head mindlessly. Then do the same motion with intention, focusing on your hips and pulling the energy from that source. The energy is so incredible that it will make you want to growl.

Visualization is another reason my work is so invigorating and deep. As my elbow glides over a tight muscle, I feel the source of my hips, and I visualize the muscle. I imagine the muscle fibers beneath my elbow loosening. I picture the tight areas filling with blood and oxygen. I truly visualize my client's body healing through my work. If my desire is to do deep work, I create the intention in my mind, and through the language of my body, I demonstrate confidence in my ability. Confidence is imperative for getting deep pressure to come from your body. Pressure from the *whole practitioner* is different then just deep pressure. There is a difference in touch when someone is working with intention, focus, and confidence, and giving from the source. Use your hips as your source, your anchor, and allow their power to fill your client with relief. Let your hips guide your intention, and use the strength only they can provide. You will give a completely different massage if you use your hips.

CONSISTENCY

As practitioners, we have parts of the body we enjoy working on more than others. It is important to be consistent with our efforts over the entire body, regardless of our personal likes and dislikes. We need to become full-body experts and conquer the hesitance we may feel in any one area of the body. I have experienced massages where the practitioner does excellent work on my back but seems to overlook my legs. Now, of course, in certain cases there is a focus on one area. Sometimes an agreement is made with the client to spend more time on an area, but unless this is discussed, a full-body experience is expected.

Even if the practitioner focuses on one area, there are ways not to overlook the other parts of the body. A client might also have likes and dislikes, and it is important to understand those as well and approach the body accordingly. If you are hesitant to work on certain body parts, it is important to spend downtime practicing and building confidence.

In the beginning of my career, I was terrified of working on the neck. It was a sensitive area on my own body, and I carried that sensitivity into my work. For a time, I had practitioners focus on my neck during my weekly massage, and I began gathering tools from those experiences to bring to my own massage. I also began letting go of my own fears by receiving neck work. It is important to know how things feel on your own body and how it feels to have your muscles unwind and loosen, so you may better serve your own clients. I believe that in most cases, the weakest areas in a practitioner's bodywork are the areas they have the most issues with when receiving bodywork. After much practice, classes, and letting go of my issue regarding the neck, my work on the neck is a stronger point of my massage.

It is also important to be consistent in asking your client how his or her body is doing and what areas need extra attention. We cannot assume, even with regular clients, that we know the answer. Every time a client enters your room, you should ask about his or her body, and find out what he or she desires from each session. Some pain is consistent, but we can never assume what a client needs. Every moment, a person's body and thought patterns change. As a body changes, it is advantageous for the practitioner to be open to change and explore new techniques.

I have a client with a sore right shoulder. I have shifted my approach, and, through a combination of methods, we have been able to relieve his shoulder pain. We have also made a visible difference in his entire back. I heard his complaints, and I assured him that working other parts of his body could help release his shoulder. I worked his neck and wrist areas, realizing that they had an effect on his shoulder pain. Even more importantly, the client now realizes that different parts of his body participate in creating the pain in his shoulder. Helping the entire body will help his shoulder to keep improving. Through consistently asking your clients questions, you will unravel the mystery of their pain.

Clients must come to sessions consistently in order to get optimal results. If both you and your client put forth effort, it will be impossible for the stress to accumulate and affect the area in such a focused way. With continued work and consistency, the entire body will be at ease and take pressure off of the mind.

Finally, your mood must be consistent. You must leave behind your own troubles and remember to be thankful each time a client arrives in your massage room. Every massage is a gift, and your reward is sharing the art of healing and receiving your pay. Without your clients, you would have no practice. Every time you see your clients, be completely gracious and thankful for their arrival.

THE SLOWER THE BETTER

One of my favorite massage practitioners and dearest friends relayed to me the concept of "the slower the better." You have sixty minutes to complete your work: there is no rush. You will accomplish everything you need to in each session. Allow your strokes to be long and full of intent. You do not need to hurry a lifelong process for yourself or your client.

A slow, caring touch is a great start to any massage. Even my deepest work is done slowly. Be generous with your strokes or stretches. If you are doing a stroke or move and you see that it is working, do it three or four times more than you thought you might. There is no hurry. Break free from sequence and feel what the client's body needs during a session. Do not move too quickly, or you will miss the view. Let your hands feel the texture of your client's body in its entirety. Take your time.

WATCH CLOSELY

I sometimes notice that when I am working on someone's neck, different muscles in their back twitch. Some call this phenomenon "muscle fire." If I am working on a tight area, I can sometimes trace the source of some of the clients pain by watching these twitches, or fires. When working between the scapula and spine, the deltoid will move. I encourage you to watch for these signs and remember that other areas of the body will react to where your hands are.

As you work on a client's neck, you will often see their hand lift off of the table. Many times, it is these same people who complain of numbness in their hands. Witnessing the connection is amazing. If your client complains of numbness in their hands, working on the neck and shoulders will probably help take away the numbness. With persistent numbness, though, make sure your client's doctor is aware of the condition. While working on the neck, you might also see the lower back tighten, because lower back pain and neck pain are directly related.

The interconnectedness of the body provides good reason to embrace the body as a whole and to be fully present for sessions. The body will tell you where to go and what to do, if you listen and watch closely. Keep your hands moving freely, and use your eyes to closely scan all your client's reactions. The body will be an incredible teacher for you. To excel in bodywork, allow it to teach you much of what you need to know to help relieve tension in your clients.

BLEND AND ENJOY YOUR DANCE

Allow new techniques to unfold as you practice or take classes. Clients will appreciate that you are trying different methods for specific problems, whether it's over time or in one session. You will be more confident if you have a whole understanding of what helps certain areas.

A class on acupuncture taught me that some people believe that shoulder pain derives from the wrist. This is probably not true in every case, but through time and personal study, I have found that many people with tight shoulders have jammed wrists. With a little tug, they adjust. I have had success from blending this idea with my own base modality to support a client's healing. Many of my clients have said that no one else has ever gone to such measures and tried so many techniques with them—and they love it.

Once you understand how to express yourself with touch, you will learn how to incorporate the tools into a beautiful dance. Clients feel like they are getting the massage of a lifetime, which puts me up a notch in their minds and helps a solid relationship grow. It is very likely that a client who experiences new ways to relieve tension will become a regular customer. Use a style that you create through your interpretation of each modality that you take the time to learn and cherish. Develop freedom in the flow of your work by creating a massage clients cannot find anywhere else.

RHYTHM

Music and rhythm are parts of the art of massage. There is a rhythm hiding behind everything on earth. It can be fast or slow, but even the fast rhythms should have an underlying slowness. A wonderful tool in understanding rhythm is to listen to your favorite piece of music or song. Even in a "faster" song there is a stillness dancing between the melody and harmony of its tune. Clear your mind and listen to the underlying beat.

Songs with a slow, steady melody tend to put the body into a calm state of relaxation and slow the mind. If we absorb the rhythm, our breath will slow down, and our body and mind will only hear the sweet sounds of the music. Through the rhythm in music, we can learn how to create our own rhythm with our bodywork.

The heart is the core rhythm of all human beings. For nine months, we lie in the womb and listen to the beat of our mother's heart during our development. Most people have probably not had another experience so intense. We go through workdays that might seem consistent, but nine months is a long time to do something day in and day out.

Imagine being in darkness and feeling and hearing the steady heartbeat of your mother. This is the rhythm we can rediscover with our clients. When the practitioner amplifies the breath and heartbeat, the client is directed into relaxation. The body will sink into rhythms, because this is where safety is found. The rhythm will captivate a client's body and bring him back to the stillness and safety of the womb, even with more intense bodywork. A client will ease into your touch through your rhythm, and they will trust where you are going with your next touch.

My mother taught me about rhythm when I was quite young. She was always dancing around the house, playing loud classic rock music. I loved watching her. I wanted to learn how to dance, too. One afternoon, I asked my mother to show me as we stood in our living room listening to the loud music. She told me to feel the music, not just to listen to it. I was confused. She told me to just move, but I was too embarrassed and shy.

She grabbed a tape and a small boom box, no iPods then, and we went downstairs to our basement. She plugged in the music and told me not to be scared.

She turned off the lights so that she could not see me. With all of the space, I was free to move however I wanted. Mom said to first dance to the beat of the drum, then to the guitar, then to the vocals, when I was comfortable, to all of the different parts separately and let my body go. Then she told me to mix it all together and separate it however I chose. I felt each part of the song and moved to its beat. To this day, I'm known to cause a commotion on the dance floor.

I later realized that the bass drum holds the core of most music, just as the heartbeat holds the rhythm of the body. Music and dance are great tools for understanding the rhythm needed to excel in bodywork. It is not about sequences, but dancing with your hands. I invite new practitioners to ponder the connection between music, dance, rhythm, and massage. The more you can move freely in rhythm, the better your hands will glide across your clients' bodies, and the further they will sink into a relaxed state.

One of the goals of my practice is to feel the rhythms of each client's body so its harmonies and disharmonies can be uncovered. Through relaxation, the mind will help the body discover itself and awaken its potential. Sometimes this may mean putting my hand into a client's armpit to get behind the scapula to massage the subscapularis. This technique may seem invasive, but I do these techniques noninvasively and with respect. Even my deepest work is done to a slow beat. Always remember your rhythm and enjoy the dance.

4

A Professional Massage Session

SACRED SPACE OF THE MASSAGE TABLE

The daily routine of preparing a room for sharing goodness to serve the community takes special care and commitment. There is sacredness to the art of massage on many levels, none of which should be overlooked. You must be dedicated in every area, from your presentation of your space, to the way you listen to and care for clients. Create an ambiance by how you interact with your clients and the atmosphere you prepare. Take special consideration to make sure your client is comfortable. Make sure you give clear instructions to new clients on how they should get ready for the massage, from what they should wear to how they should lie on the table.

When working with clients, always bring them to the room and make sure you understand their concerns. Ask them if they need to use the restroom or if they would like some water. Ask them if the room temperature is comfortable. Make sure you are attentive to their needs every time they come to your space. It is important to see your work fully and not overlook any opportunity to create a wonderful experience for yourself, your client, and the community.

PREPARING THE ATMOSPHERE

Again, there is sacredness to the space where massage is given. From the moment you enter the massage room, your focus should shift to creating the proper atmosphere for your client, clearing the space with healing thoughts for both of you. Your work is meditation. It is a place to express your passion. You have succeeded: a client is coming to receive your work. Embrace the moment and enjoy.

Prepare yourself for the client's grand entrance. As Shakespeare wrote, "All the world's a stage," and your stage should be set with healing energy. The client is about to enter your theater, and the two of you will perform a dance. The session is for both to enjoy. Your artistic ability will thrive. Enjoy being the lead performer with your client by making a beautiful play.

Sometimes burning sage or incense helps the process of preparing the atmosphere. As the smoke spreads, envision it as good energy reaching every corner of the room. If you light candles, think of them as burning away any bad vibes from the air, and the source of the flame as giving you fuel. Create a room that gives you strength and helps you feel good. As you put the sheets on your massage table, think of your client relaxing.

Of course, provide the perfect lighting and temperature. I use heated table covers in the winter, and they are a huge hit with clients; some clients even like them in the summertime with the air conditioning. A shivering body does not make for a good massage. I actually carried a heated blanket with me to house calls to improve my service. Also, I suggest choosing relaxing background music, without words.

Before your client arrives, make sure you are fully present for the lessons you are about to receive and share with the body in need before you. A fine space has been created, and, consciously or unconsciously, your client will notice the attention you've given to your working atmosphere. Agree to give your clients a healing massage, but do not agree to take on their pain or become wrapped up in their issues. Remember the energy maintenance I talked about in previous chapters. Be present, and help your clients reach the healing lifestyle they deserve.

I have decorated my rooms in a simple manner to create a homey and relaxing space. High-quality items, which I found at a discount store, hang on the walls. I was able to get very expensive mirrors and wall hangings at eighty percent off. I bought nice, dark wood tables from a discount store. The higher-end wall decorations make the tables look more elegant. I have had clients ask where I bought such gorgeous tables, and they were amazed at where they were purchased.

I keep my anatomy charts in the hallway, but even they are framed in nice wood. With the help of one of my practitioners, I chose artful charts called "Bodies in Motion," so the pictures serve as art and as a tool to answer client questions. A small lamp gives each room soft light, and I have candles surrounding the room for use in the winter when it is dark for my last few clients. There is nothing more beautiful for lighting than candles. They exude relaxation.

I have been to undecorated massage rooms, and their plainness took away from the experience. Personally, I do not like entering a massage room covered in charts. They make me feel like I'm going to a doctor's office. Also, I stay away from symbols or anything that has hidden meaning; I keep those items for the privacy of my home. I learned early on that such items might offend clients and take away from their experiences.

I came to this conclusion after an experience selling cars. My boss came to me and asked why I was wearing a cross on my coat. Someone gave me a small cross to wear for good luck while selling cars. The owner of the car dealership was Jewish, as were many of the people coming to purchase cars. He told me I was free to wear the cross, but he said it might hinder sales from people with other strong religious beliefs. I respected him and his beliefs, and I did not want religion to be a distraction for the customers. I felt I was the community's best choice as a car salesperson, and I did not want to hinder those of any religious background from buying a car from me.

I do not utilize tools or props in my massage; I use nothing but touch. I might use something for heating or cooling, but I don't use crystals or anything of the sort with *new* clients. On my first visit to a practitioner, she dangled a crystal over my face with her eyes closed. I am not sure what she was doing or where the crystal came from, but I never went back. She did not ask me how I felt about crystals or give me any information about what she was doing. If those types of items are introduced, they should first be discussed with the client. Do not enter into too many things with the client on the first several visits. Unless time reveals something different, keep things as simple as possible so clients can relax and rejuvenate.

THE CLIENT APPEARS

It is a blessing to be a massage practitioner and have a client within reach. When he or she walks through the doorway, do not hesitate to show your excitement for sharing your art. I have seen some clients every week for years. I am so excited and thankful to see them week after week that I always greet them with cheer and appreciation. I am honored to work with them and realize in return that they support me financially. It is a very sacred exchange. My mood shifts as they walk in the door. It is time for me to be fully present and unveil my art. Doing massage is a true gift, because it forces you to ground yourself and focus on the moment. It is very important to remember to be thankful for each massage.

The use of several key questions can make your clients comfortable and lets them know that time is theirs as soon as they enter the room. My favorite question to ask is "How is your body today?" Others are, "What is your ideal massage for the day?" and "Are you ready to relax?" On days that you forget, your client might even surprise you by supplying the information without you even having to ask, and some might even ask why you did not ask these key questions.

Starting with key questions will also help you put your mind in the right space as you hear yourself offering up your service. Let the clients know that you are there to serve and accommodate their needs. Listen closely to your client's wishes and allow time to cover any area mentioned in greater detail. On occasion, to get my point across that it is the client's time, I jokingly say, "If you want me to massage your toe for an hour, I will." I find humor to be the greatest way to keep things simple. Smiling and laughter are great tools to begin relaxation.

Allow your client to dictate the massage, yet feel free to communicate your ideas on the best way to reach those goals. In the case of lower back pain, for example, you may want to let your client know that you might also work the glutes, hamstrings, neck, and abs to help release the lower back. If necessary, give a brief description as to why those areas often help relieve the lower back. Make it clear what work you might do to help attain the goal of pain relief. This will begin the process of your client seeing the body as a whole.

When your clients begin asking questions, respond by promoting the concept that the body can heal itself. Begin opening their minds to this beautiful truth. Let them realize that they have the power to make decisions to uphold a healthy state. Let your client know that you are a team in attaining optimal health, by offering your continued support throughout the process. I keep in mind that if we were meant to do all of our healing work on our own, we would all live on separate little planets. People need touch and the care of bodywork. You simply cannot massage your own body in its entirety.

Also, rubbing a knot for a client week after week will not help the client's body to relax completely. We cannot forget the body as a whole. It is most important to achieve a state of total relaxation so the client can release tension. As sessions continue, take notes and mention concerns from past sessions. Ask how things worked out. The client will be impressed by your memory and will appreciate your interest.

When clients ask you how you are doing, remember it is their session, not yours. Through my experiences, I have learned that no matter what is going on outside of the massage room, I should enjoy my work and leave my problems at the door. As much as massage is a mini-vacation from stress for a client, it is also for you as a practitioner. It is your work, art, and passion, all of which some people never truly get to experience at their place of work.

SURRENDERING

Surrendering is an important art form to even begin to understand, and it takes much practice. It means different things to different people, but the end result will be similar. Listen closely to what your client says and how it is being said, but just as importantly, you must trust that you will be able to interpret what goes unsaid as well. Remember your intuition. Believe in your feelings when approaching your client. Allow yourself to surrender to these feelings. Allow the client to grow toward understanding at his or her own pace. Meet your clients at the level of truth where they are comfortable. Always remember, listening is a key of life and business. Be conscious of your clients' connection with themselves.

You are seeing the end result of a mere moment of your clients' choices and journeys. The body holds its own solutions to proper healing, which will only be revealed through surrender and commitment on the part of your client. The process of healing will only go as far as the client desires, based on the revelations they have in sessions and have had in their lifetime. All we can do is marvel at our own revelations and unconditionally enjoy clients' discoveries.

MASSAGE IS THE BEST THING EVER

"Energy flows where attention goes," a friend once said to me. As you enter the session, review in your mind everything you have learned in your training, from your experiences, and about the client. Keep your mind open to new possibilities. Your full potential as a bodyworker is always inside of you, and you are capable of tapping into that power and ability each time you go into the massage room. We cannot see electricity, but we have light. Tap into the electricity of the universe, and let your hands be lanterns of healing. Just before you lay your hands upon the body before you, clear your mind and allow your intuition to take over.

The skin is the body's largest organ, and beneath it lies our internal organs. The epidermis is constantly sending messages about our environment to the brain. It covers us with sensations. Every touch is absorbed. While feeling your client's body, quench its thirst for contact with kindness.

Flow with the energy that surrounds you, part of which you helped to create at the beginning of your day. The energy is the dance of a billion molecules, and the massage is a picture you are painting by concentrating that energy into the brushes of your hands. The client's body is a canvas, and the soothing oils are the paint. Find your rhythm, enjoy your dance, and help the client sink into relaxation and healing. Massage is wonderful. It is your work, and you are free to express yourself every session. Make every session the best massage ever.

THE MOST IMPORT PIECE OF MASSAGE ROOM ETIQUETTE

Be mindful: your clients' massage time is their own. We have five senses. Four of the five have two pieces, but they all play a role in our ability to communicate. We have two eyes, two ears, two nostrils, and two hands—but only one mouth. We only have one tongue, and we should use it wisely. It is the rudder of the boat, steering the ship.

In the massage room, you should remember to be quiet. Speak when you are spoken to, and when you speak, keep it short and simple during the session. Remember, use caution and clarity when dealing with other people and their emotions. Like a flower patiently waiting to bloom, allow the relationship to unfold at its own pace and in its own way.

Remember that you are in a business relationship. Though our office is different than most, it is important to have boundaries. Again, be silent unless you are spoken to, and use your words wisely when the client initiates conversation. Help the clients on your table learn how to be still and quiet so they can rejuvenate and better enjoy life. People really come to enjoy their massages, so allow them an hour of relaxation.

YOUR WORDS ARE PART OF THE SESSION

I always tell my practitioners to begin with a positive statement about their clients before they give an alternate response. For example, I might say, "Your body responds well to massage; it will be no time before the tightness in you shoulder goes away." It is okay to acknowledge a tight shoulder, but first, take note of the wonderful progress being made in their sessions.

I regularly see a woman who has very bad lower back pain. She is in her early fifties and has run marathons, skied, succeeded in business, and led a very full life. She has had operations on both feet, had surgery on her knee, sustained severe falls, and more. As we worked together, she was noticing a difference, but I sensed she wanted things to move along more quickly. It seemed she wanted to begin running again, but her lower back pain was still a bit too much.

I reminded her how wonderful her body has been to her and how much it has accomplished. I let her know the massage was doing great things for her body. I let her know it deserved this time to relax after many years of hard usage. She has only been receiving bodywork for a couple of months and wanted to change a body that took fifty years to tire.

After realizing her body has been good to her, she giggled and said, "You know, I have had a great life." She went on to say that she understood it would take time and realize she was lucky to be in the shape she was in presently.

I replied, "Now it is time to give back to a body that has given you so much."

She agreed, and we are making progress.

My ideals for positive feedback were reassured by studies done by Masaru Emoto. I feel that his studies clearly show how words and feelings can have an effect on people. Mr. Emoto's work provides factual evidence that human energy, thoughts, words, ideas, and music affect the molecular structure of water, the very same water that composes over seventy percent of a mature human body and covers the same amount of our planet. Water is the very source of all of the life on this planet, and its quality and integrity is vitally important to all forms of life. (You can find out more about Emoto's work at www.masaru-emoto.net.)

Emoto's studies have shown how cruel comments and different types of music affect the molecular structure of the water. By freezing water and taking a photograph of the structure, Mr. Emoto has shown that the energy of comments and music directly affected the water's crystallization. The crystallization that occurs in the test shows the effects of words on matter. Beautiful crystallization occurs with words like "love" and "compassion." Negative words cause the formation of oddly shaped, dark crystals.

Our words make a difference. Our bodies are mostly made up of water, so cruel comments might also harm our bodies. Similarly, the collection of negative thoughts will have negative effects on the human body. Share positive words with your clients. People hear enough about what is wrong: make your massage about what is right!

Through our thoughts and words, we change the makeup of our bodies. Massage provokes relaxation and satisfaction. With bodywork, we help clients conserve their energy so they can better enjoy life. After all, life is too short to be tight. Along with your massage, your words do matter, and they will have an effect on your client's body.

THE BITTERSWEET END

The end of your session is by no means the end of healing. The effects will ripple out into the world and affect all of your client's relationships. Your client has set aside a time for moments of complete rest, far away from reality.

The day is full of experiences, and in the moments of massage, there is a time of reassurance, a peak among many valleys and plateaus. This type of relaxation is necessary for optimal survival. It will probably be their quickest hour of the week. Help it be enjoyable until they leave your space. When the client is preparing to leave the room, find a phrase to help them feel the difference.

Initiate relaxed feelings at the end of your massage with your words. I always ask clients "How do you feel?" or "Isn't massage awesome?" so they pause after my work and realize they can feel a difference. Your words act as a doorway, letting the body and mind know that massage is a relaxing time.

Sometimes I say, "Feels great, doesn't it?" or "Ah, you feel better now. Do you feel the difference in your shoulder?" Reassure them that this time is helping their bodies and that there is no need to feel guilty for spending money on feeling good.

When a client leaves, tell them to pay attention, because they will notice a big difference when the massage settles in about a half hour. This helps the brain begin having positive thoughts about what is still happening after the massage. Many clients do say they did not feel the difference the last time until about a half hour later, just as I had mentioned. I truly believe it takes time for the mind to catch up to the shift that occurs during massage. The mind hops off the table in a new body session after session, and it takes time for the client to adjust and make changes.

Positivity helps clients heal themselves, and they will notice the effect of your work. Validate any concerns that they may express during this time, and give positive feedback. Be a catalyst for a positive revelation of the body's ability to be well and the greater understanding of oneself.

Take Notes on the Session

Remember, in order to recall the smaller details of the session, take notes immediately after the client leaves. Clearly write down the problem areas you found. If there was any exciting news the client shared, write it down so you can ask them the following week. Similarly, if the client is struggling with something, ask them how things are going. Take note of the changes your felt throughout the session.

Write down any goals the client mentioned or suggestions you may have given. It will be a great tool, not to mention interesting, to have a written record of your client's journey.

RIPPLE

If I massage my client, John, he will go home a happy man. His body will feel relaxed and rejuvenated. As he drives home in his new relaxed state, perhaps he questions such a stressed-out world. The traffic seems calmer on his way home than it did when he drove to our appointment.

When he arrives at his house with his massage buzz, he brings more zest for his wife, Mary. John's happy smile gives Mary a warm, cozy feeling in her heart, making her smile too. Mary feels especially well because John came home in such a good mood, and she passes more joy on to their children.

We must keep in mind this ripple effect. Our work truly does spread like a disease, but in this case, it's not disruptive. Our profession has the potential not only to change the lives of our clients, but also to benefit their friends, their families, and society at large.

No matter what is going on in my life, when I enter Freedom Massage, I remember that each session is an opportunity. The more smiling massage receivers floating around, the better the planet. And keep in mind that the happier your clients are through your practice, the more referrals you will receive—and the more people you can offer the gift of relaxation and joy through massage.

The more you focus on your clients during their appointments, the more you will see each body as unique and beautiful. Focusing on that special time will improve your chances of having your clients multiply. Not to mention that you will receive more from your sessions and will grow as a person. I have heard more than one of my clients say that I treat them like they are the only one on the planet. Every time they come in, they can trust that I will give them a high-quality massage along with a cheerful smile and heart.

Remember, John will not only go home with a smile, but his smile may cause his wife, a co-worker, or a friend to start coming for massages as well. Perhaps your smile will provoke a smile in them. Every smile we see in return makes our own smile even deeper. Every moment of your day can be used more wisely if it is done with the focus and intention of having a thriving professional massage practice.

BECOME BETTER EVERY SESSION

Take time to reflect on the entire session. This will help you benefit from the shared time and improve your service skills for the next time. Clients can be vessels that carry us to the shores of our potential. Reviewing the feelings and emotions created by the experience can help further your abilities.

Be careful of your interpretations of the moments, thoughts, and feelings shared. What you think of your client might actually be a reflection of something deep within yourself, or it might be something that you can truly understand because of your shared experiences.

I realize my clients are catalysts for my growth. Your clients are wonderful bundles of information and lessons, even if some are more difficult to deal with than others.

MASSAGE IS A TEAM EFFORT

If you do not connect with a client and have given the matter some thought, is it okay to let them go. I have created a practice where the practitioners are continually discovering each other's strengths and weaknesses. As a team, we know how to help clients. If you have a client with whom you are not connecting or are unable to make progress, you should have other resources so that the client still receives the necessary bodywork.

The virtue of integrity will serve you as well in business as it does in life. One of the ways to help uphold the integrity of massage is by unconditionally helping people to get massage appointments. In my personal practice, if I could not see a client, I always referred her or him to someone I trust. The most important thing is that the client receives quality bodywork. If my appointment book is full, my first desire is to see that the client receives a massage. It is the massage professional's duty to make sure the community receives bodywork in a timely manner. Your clients will appreciate the confidence you show through your desire to help them be served—even if it is not by you.

By choosing to believe in my art and fellow practitioners, I make sure our art gets shared. I now have a community of fellow massage practitioners who also refer business to me. If more of us referred clients, the massage profession would grow, and healing would spread more quickly. I believe that if you are truly doing things for the good of those around you, good things will come your way. By being a true professional and supporting other professionals and clients, you will be blessed twofold. Integrity also means putting the client first, always deepening your understanding of bodywork, and being passionate about your work.

Instead of struggling and not giving them your best work, you must support your clients and help them find someone who better meets their needs. Though you are letting go of one client, you will be making room for many more who will bring out your strengths. You will be surprised at the amount of calls you will receive because of your honesty.

If you are part of a community of practitioners, this is easy. If you are on your own, get out and meet practitioners whose strengths complement your areas of lesser expertise. Meeting other practitioners will also help with energy maintenance and keep your stress levels down. Dignify your work by surrounding yourself with people you enjoy working on.

In the beginning of building my practice, my first employee was the complete opposite of me. This situation was perfect for complementing our bodywork and for training practitioners. Whenever a client came through the door, we could tell if they were a specific-need client or a work-over client.

I was the heavy hitter and was considered more of the work-over practitioner because of my deep, all-encompassing massages. My peer preferred working on more muscle-specific cases and with people who intellectualized massage. We would sometimes even share clients, because we knew the other person would have a completely different approach.

Perhaps switching clients was needed for a session or two so that they could reach a fuller healing potential. Remember to accept your areas of lesser expertise, because your strengths need you.

5

Scheduling and Rescheduling Clues

SCHEDULING

Plants grow best if you routinely water them on the same day and at the same time each week; they get into a rhythm. Similarly, scheduling bodywork should get a client, and therefore his or her body, into a rhythm. The best way to battle pain cycles is with consistency, and you should explain this to your client. Pain cycles may need shorter increments between sessions so that they can be broken.

Remember that your client has been accumulating these stressors for many years, so it will take continual effort, and perhaps a couple different modalities, to undo what took years to create. You cannot rectify pain that has accumulated through a lifetime in one hour. If you are fortunate enough to do so, chances are that the aliments may come back unless pain cycles are broken and the cause of pain is rectified.

Our body uses stress to get through challenging situations, but prolonged stress will wear on the human body. As stated in the *Tao-te ching*, "High winds do not last all morning. Heavy rains do not last all day," and a body running on high all day will surely crash. Massage is one of mankind's greatest tools in combating stress. Let's face it: we live in a world where stressors are difficult to avoid. Our body combats environmental stresses, such as climate, and a variety of elements seen and unseen.

Massage is a key element for achieving optimal health, and this should always be in the forefront of your mind when discussing scheduling with clients. Massage will break the cycles of stress, and the bodyworker should make clients aware of the importance of regular bodywork.

For these reasons, you should not hesitate to ask clients when they would like their next massage. You are not selling something. You are not in a position to be pushy and aggressive. You are gathering people and sharing your massage; you are helping to heal a nation. Your hands are delivering a work of art, an ancient practice that Americans are only beginning to appreciate. It is getting harder to argue the undeniable power of touch, as there is much scientific study supporting its benefits.

Leave brochures and pamphlets with articles from reputable publications around your office. Many people will appreciate written proof. After progress is made, a client will have a better idea of how regular the sessions should be to maintain relief. Ideally, clients should come every week or more to achieve optimal health, but for some this is not financially possible, and those people should simply come as often as they can.

It is important to keep client options for appointments limited. If you give too many choices, it will get confusing. It might unconsciously cause a client to question your abilities if you seem not to have any clients. I usually offer two times on two different days after I find out whether they want evenings or mornings. I try to keep my appointments in clusters with fifteen-minute breaks. When I was building my client base, I was more inclined to spread out clients, but I've slowly brought it to a point where I will have an 11:00, 12:15, and then a 1:30 for the day. You are the mind behind the scheduling: be strong and create the schedule you desire.

One of my teachers said he used to offer new clients one appointment day and time. He laughed and said he had lots of time, but he wanted people to think he was in demand. When he would not waver from the 3:00 PM time slot, people were more likely to take his appointment. He said it added value to his work. People who valued his time would be accommodating.

In the beginning, I suggest you offer a few flexible options. If you want to see them and have the time, extend another option after you hear what times work for them. I suggest that you value your time as well as your clients. I remember what my teacher said, and I realize that people who value my time will work with my schedule and not make too many demands. Considerate clients are important in order to last in the business of massage.

By putting together a harmonious schedule filled with clients, you will change and enrich many lives. Scheduling your clients regularly gets them into a rhythm and helps them maintain it, and their bodies and overall pain management will benefit. To break pain cycles, regular bodywork is important.

Also, there is a benefit in creating a consistent schedule, because working on a familiar body is a bit easier than running your hands over a new landscape. It takes more energy to get to know a new body than to work with someone you have already had your hands on. In turn, the practitioner will have a better idea of what the week will bring and will not be as concerned with finding clients every week. There is a benefit in creating a consistent schedule for the practitioner and the client. A schedule should be rich with clients the practitioner enjoys and consistency everyone involved can count on.

Scheduling New Clients

First and foremost, if you have a message from a client on your voicemail, you must return their call as soon as possible. You should even be passionate about returning calls quickly. Oftentimes people looking for a therapist will call several people in hopes they will find an appointment. Also, usually they want a massage promptly. There were many days I would be very available to answer the phone and I would be flexible. I tried to get to peoples' homes as soon as I could. When I was doing house calls, I recall a time I could only smile as my hands were on the client as other practitioners finally returned her calls. I remember being at someone's home and their answering machine was turned up, and there was an apologizing voice wanting the client's business, but I got there first. When a new client calls for an appointment, make sure you get as much contact information as possible. Do your best to be friendly and positive. Make sure the client gets all the information they need to assure them you are the best candidate to give them a massage. Schedule the client, and again, get as much information from them as you can during this call. Make sure, if it is possible, you see the client before someone else has a chance.

ASSUME THE CLIENT IS REBOOKING

You never want to ask a question when the answer could be no. Do not ask, "Would you like to reschedule?" Instead, say, "When would you like to come back: next week or in two weeks?" Why wouldn't your client rebook? You just gave them one of the best massages of their life. If the client truly desires optimal health and relaxation, they will make arrangements and figure out solutions to make sure they can get massaged as much as possible. In fact, I believe most clients should be asking how often they should come. (I will help you answer that question in a moment.)

You should suggest coming back next week or in two weeks, but tell them not to go any longer than a month. If the client waits more then a month, it will give them too much time to undo the work you have done in your session. Remember, massage is a means of preventive health. Believe in your work.

Realize that you are providing an important service that can help the client attain a healthier lifestyle. Although many people have insurance to pay for healthcare, what about if the client has lost income due to the illness? It is important to realize that we can help prevent disease. In the long run, clients will spend less money preventing illness than paying for an illness.

You are not asking your clients to book a dentist appointment without Novocain, but to take a mini-vacation from stress. Help clients understand that they deserve to feel good. By sharing our own successes and experiences, we will help our clients realize that the physical effects of stress can be overcome with massage.

As a practitioner, you are not too busy until you have twenty clients a week and see the same faces coming in regularly. Remember clients will benefit from your services and get them into a rhythm. Do not forget to call new clients a couple of days after their first session and see how they are feeling, whether they rebook or not. It is important to have a sincere interest in the progress of your clients. Your clients will appreciate this special care.

Massage works, and people should want to come every week. Explain that a massage costs less than a dinner for two and leaves the body feeling blissful. Those who think they cannot afford it even monthly should still come as often as possible. People who do not reschedule simply do not yet fully understand the many benefits of massage and its direct link to preventive healthcare. Our bodies are a great investment. We put gas in our cars and keep them well maintained, but the vehicles we call our bodies are our greatest assets in life.

How Often Should I Come?

If your clients are serious about a healthier lifestyle and are ready to achieve a more relaxed body, they may ask you, "How often should I come?"

Ask them, "How often *can* you come?" You may be surprised at the answer, because many people will let you dictate how often they come and will actually listen to your suggestions. When it first happened to me, I felt like I was in heaven.

People want our permission. There is still not enough education about massage, and it is looked at as a luxury in many circles. People instinctively know that massage is good for them, but I do not think that we as a society are used to feeling good. People seem to think you have to work hard to accomplish good things, and massage is not in this category.

You want clients to come as often as their schedules allow. Do not do clients a disservice by *not* offering them weekly appointments, as the benefits will be incredible. If they suggest monthly appointments, have them consider weekly or bimonthly for the first couple of months. Frequent massages will help the body combat stress with full force, and the client can truly see the benefits of massage. It is best in the beginning to go in running and meet the stress head-on.

After weekly massages for a month, your clients and their bodies will have a new understanding of the many benefits of massage. The benefits will be undeniable. After several weekly visits, the client will be able to gauge how often they want to come. Remember, to break pain cycles and to attain deeper states of relaxation, the body must keep in rhythm with bodywork.

Ideally, we would get massaged every day. Once a week is probably the best option, but I see people every two weeks as well. One month is the most amount of time I would leave between sessions. Shorter increments between sessions are best. The body and mind will anticipate every visit.

It is okay to guarantee that your clients will feel a difference with regularly scheduled treatments. They will. While building my business, I would guarantee that my first massage would make a difference, or it would be a free session. Your success depends on your belief in the healing benefits of massage.

MAKING THE MOST OF CANCELLATIONS

Sometimes emergencies arise. Unexpected events are what make life so interesting. The key to success is taking advantage of the curveballs that are thrown at you. If a client cancels, stay positive. Maintain your composure and reschedule the appointment right when the client calls to cancel. Express your disappointment at not getting to interact with your client, but also express a heartfelt understanding of his or her personal needs.

If you do this, there will be fewer cancellations as the weeks progress, because you are yielding to the flow. Realize that life has a different plan for you for that slot of time; everything is as it should be. Perhaps someone with a greater need will call, or you can use the time to reflect on yourself and enhance your business in other ways.

Accept what life brings you, even if initially it seems bad or out of sync with your expectations. It won't always be easy, but you will find that a positive outlook will help you accomplish more with the time you have throughout the day. Negativity takes a tremendous amount of energy and wastes a surprising amount of time. Use the gaps in your day for goodness, and good things will come. Believe that the cancellation is in everyone's best interest.

To make sure this process happens smoothly, provide a written policy to all new clients that clearly states your expectations and requirements about canceling appointments. Make sure that you review these boundaries the first time a client comes to your office. It will help sustain positive energy and avoid conflicts.

It is also important to stand firmly behind your established guidelines if cancellations continue outside of the written boundaries you have set and explained. Charge applicable fees, and be fair to yourself. Consider the cancellation as time you could have been working with another client or being with family.

If the frequency of cancellations gets out of hand, perhaps a relationship needs to be built with someone else. Don't be afraid to let a client go if it is in everyone's best interest. You may be enabling your client to continue habits that are not good in any aspect of their lives. Supporting these acts of disrespect will cost you time and money in the long run. A disruption in the harmony between the two of you might also distract you from your best work. Trust in your boundaries and let the client move on. Time may bring you back together.

WHEN YOU NEED TO CANCEL AN APPOINTMENT

If a situation arises that causes you to consider changing an appointment with a client, consider the reason carefully. Use your cancellations wisely, because you are setting an example for your client and making a statement about what is appropriate. Just as your clients have an obligation to keep appointments and be on time, so do you. Your schedule should be carefully planned, and any changes or cancellations should be only after careful consideration.

Try not to wait until you are absolutely sick to cancel. If you feel illness coming on, rest and nurture your body before it happens—for yourself and your clients. If you push your body, the illness may conquer you, and you might miss even more sessions. It is better to rest for a couple of days than to be sick for a week. Honor your body. Use preventive measures like vitamins, massage, sauna time, exercise, diet, and yoga. You want to work when you have the glow and are feeling healthy.

Once you cancel an appointment, a door is opened. You plant a subconscious seed that allows the client to cancel in the future. I have watched it happen in my own practice for years. I take special care if I need to cancel any appointment, knowing it gives my client more permission to do the same.

Be sure that you have a very good and clear explanation for canceling. Be fair, honest, and respectful, but hold your professional ground. Although you are the one who needs to cancel, use the opportunity to train your client on how you like to be treated when it is necessary for them to cancel. Do your best to uphold the boundaries you have set for them. Share in a way that nurtures that positive energy flow. Try to explain your situation in a way that makes the client feel like you are still trying to keep him or her involved, because the client comes first.

For example, if you have to cancel, let your client know that you are primarily mindful of his or her own health: "Mary, good morning. I'm so sorry to have to cancel with you for your appointment the day after tomorrow. I seem to be coming down with a cold, and I would hate to get you sick as well. I've made a doctor's appointment to make sure that I get better as soon as possible so I can best attend to you. I think I'll be up to full strength by this time next week. What day and time works for you next week?"

If your hands are sore and need rest, let your clients know that you don't want to do them a disservice by doing a massage under such conditions. It's important to give your client as much advance notice of your cancellation as you can, so that they can make other arrangements for their day, just as you would hope to. Also, do not neglect to reschedule the appointment if you speak directly to your client. Remember, learn to rest *before* you are sick.

Your business and your life revolve around the work schedule you create. Your clients are the center pieces of the puzzle, but your schedule is the border holding those pieces together. It is important for this structure to fit as flawlessly as possible and for none of those pieces to be lost under the massage table.

6

Building Your Character

CHAIR MASSAGE

One of my mentors suggested I try free chair massage to get my business rolling. He was even kind enough to set up my first gig. On my first day of free chair massage, in a grocery store, I felt a bit awkward as I stood between the brown rice and the beans, trying to get people to accept a massage. In 1997 it was a bit more difficult than it is today, because massage was not as accepted or as well-known. I thought I would not be able to answer questions or that people would not want a massage. I had a hundred fears going through my mind, and every time I heard them, I would push myself to ask someone to have a massage.

Once I started getting my hands on people, it did not matter where I was; the confidence in my hands spoke my truth. There were people who would walk by and look at me as if I was from Mars and people I massaged who were not interested after I was finished. If I had let those few people bring me down, I would never have made it. I had to believe that even if I did not book an appointment that day, the energy I put out would come back tenfold when I was ready. You must keep going and keep massaging, and the right people will come if you are available and confident. Chair massage may seem awkward, but it is a great way to build your character.

A massage chair can be your greatest tool during the initial phase of your development as an expert in bodywork. You have the ability to conduct a lot of shorter sessions with a chair. Chair massage will help you to begin practicing your listening skills, create a technique for coming up with answers to a wide variety of questions, put you in touch with many different types of people, and give you the opportunity to spread the word about your practice.

Chair massage is a building block that goes beyond helping you with your confidence. It builds your body, and it gives you more strength physically and emotionally for client interactions. It is an opportunity to enhance body mechanics and overall knowledge of how to really use your body best. When first building your practice, chair massage is a valuable use of your time.

Be proactive: sitting and wishing you had a client to work on, instead of pursuing one, will not work. Simply handing out pieces of paper with your name on it does not give people the feeling and experience of what you are capable of doing for them. They do not walk away with a flyer feeling as if their lives could be better through massage. Even in your massage chair in a grocery store, you can deepen a person's understanding of massage.

Take these opportunities and let your hands show this potential client how wonderful you are and that you deserve their business. Chair massage is your chance to share your art with a stranger whose life it may change forever. How exciting! Consider chair massage to be the boot camp of your massage training.

One successful approach to improving your abilities and increasing your exposure is to offer chair massages at busy business centers or at health food stores. This creates a circle of giving and receiving. To receive clients, we must practice the art of giving. Throughout your career, what you choose to give to the community will likely be returned to you tenfold in the success of your business. Your business will eventually be rewarded at many levels as you share your abilities with your community. It is also aids with the building of character for everyday life.

Once you determine what kind of clients you want to work with, consider the places that potential clientele might frequent, and set up chair massage at those types of locations. I have met many new clients at holistic food stores, which have been my most productive means of adding to my client base. Another option is visiting local businesses during the lunch hour. Try setting up at your gym if you desire to find health-conscious clients. If you work out of a chiropractor's office and are not busy, do free chair massages in the waiting room to meet more clients.

In these sessions, you can work on your character and improve how you interact with people in a professional situation. During these short encounters, you can practice defining who you are as a practitioner. If used and interpreted wisely, these sessions will not be as intense as a full-body massage, but they will give you an opportunity to learn a great deal about more clients and about yourself.

Chair massage can help you learn to describe how you feel about massage therapy and how to better present your knowledge of your art's many benefits. Why is massage valuable in your life? How has it changed you and your health? Practice key phrases and see how people respond. Practice how to best to explain the concept of breaking pain cycles with massage. This is the most obvious result of our work, and it is something people will easily respond to and grasp. Understanding pain cycles is a great tool when explaining the beauty of touch.

By touching many body types in an hour, you will feel the different sizes, shapes, and textures of humans, and you will learn how to adapt your hands, approaches, and emotions accordingly. You will begin to experience the many beautiful landscapes of the human body.

During these interactions, you will most likely talk about the benefits of massage, your experience, and your education. You will learn from these potential clients, and you will begin to build more confidence. Plus, it is also a wonderful way to practice energy maintenance.

As you gain confidence and strength in your abilities, approach each potential client about continuing on their massage path to wellness. Bring along your scheduling journal and try to book as many appointments as you can on the spot. This is an effective way to generate business. Chair massage is your chance to spread the word of massage and your practice. It is an opportunity to educate your community.

It was once said, "There is no such thing as luck. There is opportunity met with preparation." Chair massage will help you realize the truth of this statement. If I get one client through chair massage who works with me for a year, then it has been a success. Keep in mind, you should always be polite and not pushy. It is important to seem eager—but not desperate. The right people will come into your life and your practice if you are simply enjoying life. Begin building your character through the use of a massage chair.

MASSAGE PARTIES

Another great way to use chair massage as a marketing tool is to offer parties. Tell your clients that you will bring your massage chair to their home for a massage party. There is no charge for the party! All you ask is for the host or hostess to inform guests that tips will be appreciated.

Here, you have created a win-win situation, because the client has a great party, and you get paid to do marketing. It will give you an opportunity to talk to new people about massage in a relaxed atmosphere. Get your clients involved in helping your business grow, and give the perk of a free massage party! Get out there and massage!

FREEDOM MASSAGE PHILOSOPHY

I had a client who came into my office with a really tight right shoulder. Her shoulder was hurting her badly, but she had no idea why. As I worked on her, there was anger in her tone when she said it really hurt. As the session continued, she went on to tell me she was getting a divorce. She continued to express her anger, and the tightness in her shoulder released so dramatically that she herself realized that it was caused by the stress of her divorce.

Once she had the space to acknowledge what she was feeling, through touch and her realization, a lot of her pain melted away. This session was great because we made a huge amount of progress in only one hour. It is important to remember that some progress takes time, but in this session, I was lucky to have a client who quickly realized the cause of the pain she was experiencing. When given the space, a client's desire will unfold the truths of their bodies.

I believe we will never truly know the cause of a client's pain as well as they will, because we do not dwell within the walls of their minds or bodies. Consciously or unconsciously, your clients know their bodies better than anyone else, so don't be afraid. With care and permission, ask questions about your client's experiences and feelings in certain problem areas. If someone asks me, "Why is that so tight?" I often respond by asking, "How does it feel to you, and why do you think it is tight?"

I believe a muscle is tight not only from activity or inactivity, but also from emotions and heredity. Heredity runs deep throughout our bodies; it is the history of all our ancestors, creating the final result of who we are today. Our past experiences, and even those of our families, claim a part of our body's makeup. It is habit and repetition.

The body is a grid of the activity and emotions of our experiences and our mind, sometimes carrying all the way back to our childhood. I believe many different emotions and physical traits are passed on through the generations. Interpreting the cause of pain can be a tricky matter. I have learned to help my clients discover the source of their pain, but I believe it is really up to the client to declare.

If I had gotten caught up in the pain of my client with the sore shoulder and tried to explain the fundamentals of the body, this may have distracted her from truly discovering the cause of it. I would have diverted her from the truth of her issues by telling her that her right deltoid was tight from carrying her purse or maybe from holding a phone incorrectly. In this case, and probably many others, these reasons were not true.

Giving too much information as you diagnose someone's painful regions during sessions might override the other levels of understanding and acceptance of that pain within the client. The feedback that you give, which might escalate as you and your client become more familiar, should be carefully considered.

Realize that your feedback is merely an opinion or an answer based on your perception. We are not doctors. Help the client see the body as a whole, and help them realize that their pain is the result of a cause.

Again, pain is the body's last cry for help. We as practitioners have no access to the inner workings of the client's mind, nor have we spent every moment with them. Therefore, we are not in the position to determine the cause of a clients' pain in its entirety. Simply focusing on relieving pain is not always the answer; understanding the pain, so that it will not continue, is.

It is important that the client not become dependent on the practitioner's opinion of what is wrong. Instead, I believe the practitioner should help the client learn body awareness and how to be in tune with his or her own body.

I have seen numerous clients after another practitioner had given them an earful about their symptoms. Clients become convinced they are tight messes with specific problems, which are usually made out to be quite horrible. Massage practitioners often point out symptoms and certain muscles, and they name them as the cause of their clients' pain. This choice is taking them all the way to the last chapter of the book before they read the first page. I believe it is also an unfair summary. We need to help the client get back to the introductory paragraph and allow them to give their own analysis of the book. Remember, it is our goal to help the client discover the cause of his or her pain. As your clients experience their bodies relaxing, they will become more aware of their bodies as a whole. The greatest gift I believe I give my clients is allowing them the space to discover their bodies and understand the body's dynamics in whatever language or way they desire. Again, I do not rush their process, I merely hold the door open.

As massage practitioners, we have the opportunity to create an ocean of peacefulness. We are part of a profession unlike any other in the world. In many walks of life, touch has been lost; in our art, it has been found. We are like all the droplets of water coming back to the ocean, keeping it full—giving life to the entire planet.

The group consciousness cannot reach its potential if the members of the group are not fully participating. Each of us plays a subtle role in the body known as humanity. If we acknowledge this role and uphold our integrity as individuals, we can be a positive force for ourselves and others.

Through this acknowledgment, we help keep the simplicity and joy of being human in the highest regard. Touch awakens the body's desire to heal. We are in a position to provide a doorway into preventive measures of healthcare. To help the group raise its consciousness, we must embrace our profession with our entire being. Our touch and care, if presented in a professional, artistic, and respectful way, can change the perceptions of people who do not recognize the power of touch. With the right attitude and practice, massage practitioners have the ability to be an integral part of major life changes for their clients. When the body is given healthy opportunities, such as touch, it can awake the body on many levels. An important part of the Freedom Massage philosophy is caring about and enjoying your clients. Being a bodyworker is an incredible opportunity to spread the joys and healing power of touch. It is a wonderful job to grow as a person and lead a life in a relaxed working environment. Your clients will all be happy to see you, so relish in the opportunity to make a difference.

Practice your body mechanics so that you can work without much effort, and do a dance with your client. Your massage, time and time again, can be an expression of an art practiced for centuries. Your work will help everyone who enters your massage room. Remember the ripple effect I spoke of earlier; know that you are making a big difference in your community.

Be thankful for every session and every opportunity to do what you will grow to love. Massage is an incredible gateway for self-discovery, joy, good health, and healing for all parties involved. Remember, always enjoy your clients: they are gifts! Never take such an incredible opportunity for granted, and love being a bodyworker!

REMEMBER: THE WORLD IS WORKING FOR US, NOT AGAINST US

In life, we must enjoy each moment of our lives the best we can by unraveling our minds and connecting deeply with our bodies. When we get on a train, there are people working for us. The train stops at its given time and safely takes us to the next stop. The body is our personal transportation, a personal vehicle, if we care to see it as such. When you get in a car, which was built for your driving pleasure, you comfortably drive quickly from place to place. The car industry is working for us, and they did a fine job building my car.

The whole world is working for us, not against us. It is our responsibility to understand what keeps us from seeing and experiencing the beauty of this creation. Only you can stop your dreams from coming true. There is no timeline, so things will happen as they may. It is important to see all of the things that are moving in the right direction instead of focusing on the bad. Remember the vastness of life.

7

Business/Before the Beginning

I believe much of your massage practice will be based on your intention. Before you choose what kind of client you want to work on, make sure that you work on several different types of people. My first apprentice thought she wanted to work with chronic pain sufferers and attracted many as a new practitioner. She thought it was standard. Very quickly, she became exhausted and asked me how I did so many massages. I told her that I created my ideal client base. You don't have to work with people who are in a state of chronic pain unless the work is bringing you joy.

Find out what and who feels best to you. What kind of work do you prefer? What body type? What type of personality do they have? Pay attention to how you feel with different people and begin to figure out what kind of client you enjoy the most.

You must also decide on the atmosphere you would like to work in. Before you decide if you want to work on your own or in a business, maybe you should try a little of both. What kind of practice do you want to be in? Will you do out-calls? How much money do you want to make? Will you accept tips?

Remember, you will absolutely need to become a businessperson. The tips in this book are intended to help you in that process. As a sole proprietor or an independent contractor, you will be a bookkeeper, salesperson, marketing person, receptionist, and more. Furthermore, even as an employee, you will need to have a strong foundation in all these areas. It is important to see yourself in the setting you believe you wish to be in.

By focusing and trusting your intuition, I believe you will create your ideal work environment, client base, and income. First, sit down and get some of your intentions in order, and begin making your career goals come true.

I chose the name Freedom Massage long before my business was in existence. It was July 7, 1997, to be exact. At that point, I had no idea what I wanted to do. I did know that, to me, massage meant "freedom." I would no longer be in an office working nine to five, on a car lot, and would be totally free to promote something I believed in with all my heart. I would be able to introduce a preventive care modality which would help people feel amazing. I would be in an environment without the pressures sometimes found in offices. I was free to express an art and create an income in the process. Massage brought me a sense of freedom, thus the name Freedom Massage.

I knew massage would be a gateway to something life-changing for my clients and for myself. I believed I would have an impact on the business and that I would teach other practitioners someday. I set the intention, and ten years later, I have the tools to provide. You might not know how it will all work itself out, but it is important to recognize your intentions even if you start off with two vague ideas. I also realized that I wanted to work with people who understood the importance of bodywork and loved mine. I now work with people I enjoy, and we have fun!

Remember, a focused intention to succeed is a significant part of building your practice. Everything can be set up perfectly, but without intention, your massage table will remain empty—maybe even dusty. Focus on your goals. Write them down, talk about them, tell them to strangers, sing songs about them, and think about them in the shower. This will certainly help you begin creating them.

The most important preparation in reaching any goal starts in the mind. The first step in making it through the long haul is to picture your strengths and successes in your head. It is so important to get your mind on track and have it working with you, not against you. Keep your thoughts positive, and get ready to run the marathon of massage. Believe in yourself and your dreams.

A TRUE BUSINESSPERSON

There is a difference between a great massage therapist and a great massage businessperson. My accountant told me very early on in my practice that I was an awesome massage practitioner, but that it would take years for me to become an accomplished businessperson. I did not understand what he was saying until I began to face the many obstacles related to business, from getting my business name to opening a business bank account.

I have heard a lot of names for massage practitioners; unfortunately, I have not heard many refer to us as excellent businesspeople. The most important thing to remember is to be professional. Without this, nothing else will truly help you flourish in your practice. For the good of massage, be professional. Massage school ends, and we are cast out into the world. The dream of making a prosperous life into a reality is brought to our attention quickly after graduation.

It is now time to head into the real world with real people, real joys, and—even more—real problems. This is when all of our ideas are put to the test. After emerging from the safety that a formal education provides, you will not be able to open a big book to find all the answers to the questions your work will bring forth. Though I have tried to cover many in this book, there are too many different kinds of people and too many situations to cover.

Find a mentor, someone who is already in the massage business, or a businessperson you can trust. Spend time talking with them and getting suggestions as you come across different obstacles in your practice. If your lesser talent is accounting, take an evening class in accounting or find an accountant who will be patient as you grow. Be willing to humble yourself and ask for help as you grow in the business world. Remain as fascinated with the workings of business as you are with the workings of the body.

Honestly, having your own massage business or wellness center is an incredible amount of work. As I interview a lot of practitioners, they tell me their long-term goal is to have a wellness center. There is so much work involved with having a wellness center, that sometimes you lose your art. If you plan to open a wellness center or a massage business, keep in mind that you will absolutely need to be an outstanding businessperson. I have watched many of these centers open and close in my area. It takes a huge commitment to make it work.

I run my business and still see fifteen to twenty clients a week. I continue to massage, because it is what I love to do. When I chose to expand my business and become an employer, I had to grow to love management, bookkeeping, advertising, and marketing on an entirely different level. I put myself into the position of the boss, which is very different then being a peer. It was a lesson I had to learn, and I continue to learn. It is something you cannot truly grasp until you experience it. Needless to say, it is a difficult transformation.

Make sure you know what you are getting into as you choose your practice. It has taken seven years of trial and error to get to a point where I am beginning to become a great businessperson, seven years to learn the dynamics of business and begin to realize what it means to me to be a great boss. It is a challenging process, and it takes commitment. I still have a long way to go, and there are areas of my business that still need improvement. It is a lifelong process. I think we need the existing wellness centers to be filled with excellence; only time and the commitment of a group can make that happen.

8

Useful Business Tips

NAMING YOUR BUSINESS

We need to talk plainly about the fundamentals of starting a massage business. If you are doing massage and getting paid, it is a business. Be professional, be who you are, and enjoy what you do.

Give your practice a name if you are planning to be a sole proprietor or LLC. Having a name will help make your business a reality. It is a big step in setting intention. Not only will your energy be behind your name, but you will be legal! I chose the name of my business even before I finished massage school, and I am glad I did, because I got the name that best describes my practice. Every time I hear the name Freedom Massage, it reminds of the journey to success that I have taken.

If you have a name that you like, you will need to apply for a DBA, also called an assumed, trade, or fictitious name. A DBA filing is an official public registration of a business name with either the state or local jurisdiction. You can go online and do a search for the Department of State Corporation Bureau in your area, legalzoom.com, or bizfilings.com. These Web sites will show you what names are taken, and you can set up your name in minutes. This helps set your intention, showing that you are serious about creating your own massage business. Getting a DBA will give you rights to the name, and it will prevent you from inadvertently using someone else's name.

Furthermore, check online if you plan to have a Web site, and make sure no one is using the address you've chosen. You might find that someone else is using your ideal Web site name already. This might also have an effect on what you decide to call your business. If there was another Web site named freedommassage.com, it might have changed my mind to pick the name. I would have needed to use the Web site fmassage.com, and it would have been more difficult to remember. I also would have quickly realized that someone else had already picked the name I wanted. When I tell people my business is Freedom Massage, it is easy for them to remember freedommassage.com. You will need to have a DBA name if you are planning on opening a business checking account.

Reasons to get a DBA:

1. To notify other businesses that the name is in use and to make sure the DBA you want becomes public record.

2. It is a requirement by most banks when opening a business account

3. To develop character and identity

4. Create a solid marketing theme

Get Insurance

Every practitioner should look into liability insurance, which is very important to carry. If you are independent or an employee it is important to find out what insurance you need to have to protect your business. Insurance is a necessity for your practice. In the event a lawsuit is filed against you or your practice, it could be financially devastating. Some insurance protects you in the event you are sued for *any* work you are qualified to perform as a massage therapist. A general liability insurance may also protect you against nonprofessional liability claims for what could happen during massage therapy, either on or off premises. This may include things such as property damage and legal liability related to fire damage to properties you rent. If you have employees or are an employee, note that in some cases employees must obtain their own coverage by becoming members of a insurance group and they may not be named as additional insureds.

The major providers of liability insurance for massage therapists seem to be Associated Bodywork Massage Professionals (ABMP) and the American Massage Therapy Association (AMTA). It is important for all practitioners to have liability insurance. You can go online for more information about joining one of these groups. It is worth the few hundred dollars a year to have peace of mind.

TAX ID NUMBER OR EIN

You will need a tax identification number if you are planning to start your own massage practice with employees. You can apply for an EIN online at www.irs.gov/business. Go to "Related Topics" and click on "Employer ID Numbers."

BUSINESS CARDS

I found my original business card to be most effective when I was a single practitioner. It was similar to a card a realtor might distribute: it had my picture on it and all of the necessary contact information. People like being able to put a face to the name. Keep your card concise and simple, but add a personal touch. As your business evolves, your literature must evolve also. You might eventually want to establish a logo that expresses massage.

In the beginning, it is okay to design and print your own business cards using a software program such as Microsoft Publisher. You want to be in control of the changes on business cards and have them readily available. When I was getting started, things changed quickly: everything from what I offered to where I offered it. My ideas for logos also changed, so I was happy to have my cards available on my computer to print out whatever I desired. By using a commercial printer, you are at the mercy of a company. Using your computer means that you can print on your own time schedule. Early on, I found out that it was a waste of money to pay someone until I was established and settled.

After a year or so, if you decide to get cards professionally printed, be prepared to ask a lot of questions. Find someone through a recommendation. You can always go to somewhere like Kinko's, but I prefer a more intimate setting. There are many variations of printing. You can get computer laser printing or plates, but plates are usually the highest quality. Remember, it is okay to be a student; when building a business, this is absolutely the case. Ask questions and educate yourself in every aspect of your business.

Clients who get weekly massages have an eye for quality. My business cards are now always printed on linen paper. Choose whatever feels good to you, but make it professional and crisp. Trust me, people who know different modalities will ask you if you provide them, so keep your information simple. Wordy business cards can hinder people from making a call. I believe my simplicity led to my success. I was careful not to talk above people. Keep it simple, clear, and professional.

ADVERTISING

People always ask me how I advertise, and I let them know that I keep it simple. The best advertising will be word of mouth. I have kept close track over the years, and most of the business for Freedom Massage still comes through our existing clients. I also let everyone know where they should go for a massage. It is important to talk to people and tell them what you do.

For instance, eight years ago I was doing chair massage at an event. I gave a massage to a very nice lady and told her she should come for a massage. About a month later, I was doing chair massage somewhere else, and I saw her in the distance and said hello. I asked her if she wanted another chair massage, and she smiled. She said, "The next time you massage me, I am paying." I was doing chair massage for free, and I felt it was her way of saying she would call for a massage. Weeks later, I was going to rent a movie, and I saw her again. I went up to her with yet another card and told her three times was a charm. She has been coming to me every two weeks ever since. I was persistent and willing to make myself vulnerable, which created a solid and lasting relationship.

I was massaging at yet another event, and I saw a gentleman wearing a golf shirt from the golf course across from my father's home. I went up to the gentleman and told him what a beautiful course it was, and asked him if he was a member. We began chatting a bit, and I asked him if he wanted a massage. He said not right then, but told me that his wife had been looking for someone. He briefly slipped away into the crowd and came back with his wife. I worked on her, and she loved it. Two weeks later I was at their home massaging them and another couple—not to mention the fact that it was the highest paying job I'd ever had at the time. My original contact was kind enough to give me a one-hundred-dollar tip because he thought my price was too low. How cool is that?

Advertising starts with you and your ability to talk to potential clients. Also, it is crucial to maintain a professional edge as you pursue potential clients. Remember to be persistent but not pushy. Take advantage of golden opportunities the universe will provide to build your client base. If you are doing a wonderful job and take special care of your clients, they will be your greatest advertisement.

BROCHURES

You can do a nice quality brochure on your home computer using Microsoft Publisher. Using your personal computer is a big money-saver when you are just starting out. My first brochure had my picture on it, and because of this it caught many peoples' eyes. The picture was basically my first logo. The front of my brochure showed me massaging someone, and on the inside cover I included a headshot of myself.

Keep the information in your brochure simple. Simply stating concepts is sometimes the clearest and most professional way of getting a point across. People will read bulleted lists before they read two pages of facts, and they will read more closely if they understand the language being used.

I put a short biography on the inside cover and included bullet points naming some of the benefits of massage. It is also important to include testimonials. It is okay to use friends and family for your first brochure; make sure to list their name and their occupation. I also listed my prices for one-hour and ninety-minute massages, with a brief description of both. You might also add a coupon on the brochure, or simply state, "$10.00 off your first massage with this brochure." These are the key ingredients to a money-making brochure.

WEB SITES

It is important for any business to have a Web site. To register a Web site name, you must go through the Domain Registry of America at www.droa.com. If you have someone designing the Web site, he or she should be knowledgeable on how to make this process simple. Freedom Massage gets a lot of business through our Web site. A Web site is continuous advertising at work for you—even while you sleep. Considering its value, it is an inexpensive way to advertise.

YELLOW PAGES

Advertising in the phone book is expensive, but it is surprising what an ad in the local yellow pages can still do for business. Even in a time when many people look online for services, there are still people who love the yellow pages. I picked the book specifically for my area, and it has brought new faces into our practice regularly. I bought an ad smaller than the size of a business card. It has proven itself more powerful than the bigger ad I bought the previous year, and it is worth every penny. At the very least, you need to be in the yellow pages as a single-line ad. The potential of people finding us in the yellow pages has not ceased to exist, so do not overlook it as an outreach to the community.

ACCOUNTING/BOOKKEEPING

Finding a reliable and skilled accountant is one of the most important steps in building a solid business. I believe it is one of the first steps you should take. It is best to find an efficient and trustworthy accountant through friends or family. Ask around, and even conduct interviews until you find someone you feel can help you make strong decisions. The IRS does perform random audits; it could happen to you, so you should always be prepared. It is less stressful to do things correctly from the beginning.

When I first started my business, I did not keep detailed records as I understand them now. I was a part of a random audit. The gentleman from the IRS giggled upon entering my office and said my chances of winning the lottery were the same as getting audited. Lucky me.

He explained that they did these audits to keep up with the times and to build a better understanding of the write-offs that businesses were declaring. For example, in 1980 no one was writing off Palm Pilots and things of that nature.

Preparing all the information correctly became a huge undertaking within the time restraints of the IRS. Your bank will give you records for free if the IRS requests specific items when you are being audited, but the information I needed were things I was expected to have—but didn't. These items were very costly. It was a very hard, quick lesson in bookkeeping. It was the worst summer of my life, yet one of the greatest lessons in building my business. My business suffered because I was preoccupied by trying to remember situations that I overlooked in 2001 during the summer of 2004, instead of concentrating on the present.

It takes just a few minutes a week to save you hours, even weeks, in the future. I was able to walk away with little distress due to the patience of my accountant. It was a lesson that helped me realize that I also needed a bookkeeper. My accountant was not responsible for keeping track of all of my deposits and the more integral parts of my spending—nor was it our agreement for him to do so. If you are not strong in this area, I suggest that you find a bookkeeper who can help with the smaller details of your business. I encourage you to set up these smaller details of your business from the beginning, and have a solid understanding of how your bookkeeping should look.

Here are the most important lessons in bookkeeping that I have learned over the years:

Keep all of your business dealings separate from your personal accounts. Keeping separate accounts will be a tremendous help to keep things clear. Open either a business account or a DBA (Doing Business As) personal account. Opening a DBA personal account is the least expensive and most practical option when you are just starting out, and it worked best for me. Your accountant can help with your decision.

In order for this part of the equation to run smoothly, you will need to have taken the steps previously outlined—register your business name, obtain a tax ID number or EIN, etc.

Only pay for bills incurred by the business from your business account, and your personal bills from your personal account. Save all receipts for items you've purchased or bills that you've paid for by check, and write the check number on the receipt or statement.

Create a filing system to keep track of your receipts. Label folders and put the receipts in the proper category. For instance, any checks written for advertising for the year should go in the advertising folder with the check number and amount written on the receipt or bill.

If you ever go through an audit, you might need to explain where every check went and what it was for. If you keep the receipt with the check number, you will have all the information. Then, at the end of the year, you will be completely organized. All I do now is put a big rubber band around my folders for the year, give them a kiss, and store them away. Everything is written down, plus I have copies of my bills and receipts.

Get a credit card for business only. When you need to buy something for the business, use this credit card. It is much easier to keep track of expenses this way. Keep all credit card receipts in a folder. At the end of the month, staple your receipts to the credit card statements with the corresponding purchases.

The receipt gives you proof of what you purchased. For example, if it says "Target" on your statement, then, with the added help of the receipt, you can easily show that you bought candles. Without the receipt, you have no proof that the purchase was for business, and you will be charged for that amount by the IRS during an audit.

It takes very little time at the month's end to gather the receipts for each statement, put them in order according to the statement, and file them in your business credit card file. It will be easy to explain where and why you used your credit card. During my audit, the IRS asked to see several receipts, and I was unable to present them. Therefore, the items in question could not be written off, and I had to pay past-due tax on those items, with penalties. Without the proof, you are at a loss.

Keeping track of clients and payment is crucial. Every deposit must be explainable. Every week I write down the clients I saw, the date, the type of payment they used, the check number (if applicable), and the amount paid. I use an accounting book I purchased at Staples to neatly enter this information. I add the totals for cash and checks, deposit the monies into my business account at the bank, and attach the receipt for the deposit to the list of clients for the week. As I page back through my accounting book, I can explain every dime received for every week. Also, it makes it easier to enter it into the system we use to finalize the accounting at the year's end.

The bookkeeping program I chose was QuickBooks. I prefer having a written copy and a copy on the computer. With this, I can explain every bank deposit. I now know that this is what the IRS wants to see when they audit, and it helps me keep track of my money.

The ritual of keeping track of your clients, income, and business purchases should be exciting. It helps you paint a clear picture of how you are doing and where your money is going. It also keeps you and your business headache-free. Be patient. It may take a while to figure out a system that works for you. Do not underestimate the importance of having a paper trail. Remember, if you are doing massage for a living, it is a business.

MILEAGE

If you are audited, you have to be able to explain every mile you write off: the date, where you were driving, and how many miles you drove. Mileage write-offs are consistently abused, and using mileage as a "write off" expense almost guarantees that the IRS will check your mileage records. They want to know it all.

If you are not the type of person who will remember to keep track of your mileage every day, find another solution. I regularly take my sheets to get laundered, so I go by my sheet receipts and my planner. I know that the cleaner is fifteen miles round trip. The receipts tell me when I was there throughout the year. My house calls are marked in my schedule book, so I review them every quarter. It would probably be best to write my mileage down every day, but that is not practical for me.

You should find the way that works best for you, but be consistent. Make sure you can explain everything; if you can't, it is not worth saving a few bucks only to have a headache later.

9

Pricing and Salary Advice

SELF-EMPLOYED

It takes time and experience to become a bodyworker. I was about ten years old when my Aunt Maggie began asking me to rub her shoulders. As time passed, I got better and better. I realized that my services were in demand when I began to be bribed with payment of a quarter for my work. Word spread throughout the family, and as my talent grew, so did the demand for my services. I raised my price to a dollar. My loved ones agreed to the increase, and they made me feel like a superstar, praising my abilities and raw talents.

Soon word got out to friends of the family, and they would come over and pay the fee to receive my work. It was the beginning of my practice of noninvasive, caring touch. I became acutely aware of what felt good to others and how to find a rhythm with the human body.

Similarly, when I began my practice, I priced my massages low. I was not comfortable charging regular rates, and it worked for a while. As time passed, I found some people turning up their noses at my low pricing. I was on the Main Line in the suburbs of Philadelphia, where people expected service to be priced according to quality. When I told people my price, it was almost as though they were asking themselves, "Why is she so cheap?" As time passed and my confidence grew, I felt that I deserved to increase my price, because my skills had flourished.

Your time is valuable, and so is your work. It is important to charge the right price for your efforts—and quality does come with a price. Developing a quality massage practice is like being behind the creation of a piece of music. Instead of merely following the notes of others, you create your own composition. When you take a chance on writing your own song, you will stand out instead of blending in.

It is best to establish clientele who admire your work. You are not just a logo, an advertisement, or a low price, but a service rendered with true care. If you provide excellent service in a wonderful atmosphere and attract people who admire your work, you will receive the price you deserve. If you're working on your own, don't be afraid to raise your rates as you grow as a practitioner. The clients who adore you will respect this decision.

EMPLOYER

Sometimes, I wish I could step out of my position as a business owner and work for myself. Between their salaries and tips, my employees are doing better than I was several years into my practice. I pay them an excellent wage and regularly offer incentives. Once in a while, I will give them bonuses for being helpful and excelling at their job.

One of the joys of being a small-business owner is getting to treat people the way I wanted to be treated as a practitioner working for someone else. So if you establish your own business, I suggest paying your employees more than you were making at that point in your career. Make it a win-win situation. If your employees are happy, they will help create the positive feeling needed in a growing business.

Massage is demanding work, and as a skilled practitioner, you should be paid well for your efforts. Also, as an employer, the more you share, the greater your return.

EMPLOYEE

If you choose to work for someone else, it is still important to excel in the practice as if it were your own. As a massage practitioner, you will probably be paid more per appointment than for office duties. Pursuing a full book of massage—no matter who you might be working for—is the only way you will make a living without having to deal with the burden of running your own business.

Find a salary that matches your goals, and appreciate every client the business you're working for provides, by rebooking the client. A business owner can help provide the clients and the materials, but keeping the client is dependent on your own care and skill. Always remember, although you work for someone else, it is your responsibility to create repeat business. In the long run, this effort will make your job easier and your paycheck stable.

Please keep in mind that these are my beliefs, and you should seek the advice of a professional who is an expert in dealing with this part of your business. The information in this section of the book is basic and is meant to point you in a direction you will seek yourself. I have experience, but I also have an accountant.

10

Independent Contractors vs. Employees

The question of whether you're an employee or an independent contractor has come up a lot for me over the years. In 1987, the IRS developed a list for its auditors to use to determine whether a worker was an employee or an independent contractor. It is available online and at the end of this section.

The measure of control an employer has over its workers is the determining factor. If the employer controls the results of the work and not the day-to-day performance of the task, then the worker is probably an independent contractor. Many massage businesses will have you work as an independent contractor, but if you read over the twenty questions on the IRS list, you will see that this is probably not the correct title. More than likely, they should categorize you as an employee.

If you are working for someone, I believe being an employee is your best option. The employer will pay toward your Social Security, and you will not pay a self-employment tax, which takes about a fifteen percent cut of your money in addition to the taxes you are already paying.

Your paycheck may seem bigger as an independent contractor, but do not let it fool you. It is tax-free money, and you will eventually need to reimburse Uncle Sam—by April, in fact. The amount of taxes you pay will be greater as an independent contractor than if you were an employee. You will need to get paid a considerably higher wage as an independent contractor to have it outweigh the comforts of being an employee. Independent contractors are responsible for paying all of their own taxes and keeping track of all the paperwork to support write-offs. Though you are working within the walls of another person's business, you are considered self-employed.

As an employee, you will receive a W-2 at the year's end and potentially receive money from your tax returns. The only things you are responsible for as an employee are your private clients. Employees get taxed less and as a friend of mine who is an independent contractor bodyworker discovered, you do not need to pay a lot of money at the end of the year to have your taxes done. Having an accountant prepare your taxes as an independent is costly. If you do the accounting on your own, figure into your income the hours you spend on this, to determine your *actual* hourly wage.

If you are starting a business, I suggest you look over the IRS list and decide whether you want to hire independent contractors or employees. If your business is set up with independent contractors and there is an audit, you could lose your business if everything is not done properly.

Again, I suggest finding a good accountant to help you set up a system regardless whether you are a business owner, employee, or an independent contractor in the business.

Questions Used to Distinguish Employees from Independent Contractors

If the answer to *any* of these questions is yes, the worker may, in fact, be an employee and not an independent contractor.

Does your employer give specific instructions as to how the job or service is to be completed?

Is training required for the worker to complete the job or service in a specific manner?

Is the completion of the job or service necessary to ensure the continuation of the business?

Is the worker required to perform the job or service personally?

Is the worker hired, supervised, and paid by the employer?

Is the worker required to work only for the employer?

Is the worker required to perform the job or service on the employer's premises, even though the work could be performed elsewhere?

Is there a continuing relationship between the worker and the employer?

Is the worker required to adhere to the employer's schedule?

Does the employer require regular written or oral reports?

Is the worker paid by the hour, week, or month instead of by the job or straight commission?

Does the worker pay his or her own business or travel expenses?

Does the worker furnish his or her own tools and materials?

Does the worker have any investments, such as an office or machinery, required for completing the job or service?

Can the worker realize a profit or loss based on the job or service performed?

Does the worker work for more than one person at a time?

Are the worker's services performed for the general public?

Can the worker be fired if he or she is performing the job or services agreed upon contractually?

Can the worker terminate the job or service without risk of financial loss due to a breach of contract or litigation?

Is the worker required to perform the job or service within specified hours?

11

Helpful Forms Explained

There are probably fancy computer programs you could use for some of these forms, but a pencil and paper may be a good place to start. Not only is it important to have a hard copy of all forms, but it will also save you money.

EMPLOYEE CONTRACT (EXAMPLE IN APPENDIX)

I remember the first time I signed an employee contract for massage. I was insulted. I did not understand why the business owner thought I might steal clients. Therefore, I began my business without a contract, only to learn just how important they really are. I really thought people would keep their verbal agreements with me, as I had with my employer. It worked for three years. I felt so proud and honored to have helped create a community of honest and righteous people—until one day, when it all came to an end.

An employee who worked for me left the business in an unprofessional manner. My belief in my perfect business and perfect employees was suddenly tainted. I felt my head spinning and wished I had not only a spiritual agreement, but also a written agreement. I still am a "peace, love, and happiness" boss, but now I am practical too. I have also become the businessperson I spoke of earlier.

It is important for new employees to understand your expectations as a supplier of massage. As an employer, I now realize that it is important for the employee to understand the incredible effort that has gone into your business and your ability to bring clients to practitioners.

Emotions can run wild, and lines can be blurred, which is why documentation is essential. Also, there are simple and innocent situations I have experienced where an employee misunderstood my thoughts; I now have these boundaries written down for employees so there is no confusion.

One of my rules is that under no circumstances should a client have an employee's home or cell phone number. I decided this after a new employee gave her number to a client. He called her later in the week to discuss a TV show, and she felt awkward. She immediately came to me, very upset. To avoid any questionable situations with clients and to uphold true professionalism, clients should only contact my employees through the business, unless otherwise discussed with me.

I have created a system, through a contract and a pay sheet, to help practitioners honor a code of ethics. Every week they list which clients they brought *to* my business and the clients they obtained *through* the business. The employee contract very clearly states that they are making an agreement to be professional but not take ownership of Freedom Massage clients. Does any client belong to anyone? No, but employees benefiting from a business should respect their employer's help in providing a client base, doing advertising, providing a space to work in, and taking care of the behind-the-scenes aspects of the business. If it was not for the persistence and hard work of the business owner, the practitioner may have never met the clients they work with within the wall of the business.

I believe that if employees feel strongly about socializing with clients from Freedom Massage, then they should first discuss it with me. At that time, we come to an understanding, and I feel comfortable that the practitioner is not building a private business through the fruits of my efforts. Unfortunately, my experience in many massage businesses has shown me that this can often be the case.

My favorite story to share with new employees is about my signing a contract. As stated earlier, I felt a bit insulted by the request. I read the contract and decided I would follow its outline no matter what the future entailed, believing the company I worked for would give me an opportunity to grow within their business. It turned out that my client base at this business grew rapidly. I became very comfortable rebooking clients quickly, thanks to my experience in sales and my passion for bodywork.

I appreciated the owners' efforts and realized the hardships they had overcome to build a massage business from scratch. I wanted to become more of a training practitioner; I felt I began to understand how the process of rebooking occurred. I believed I could share some of my techniques with other practitioners in the business and help it grow. I also felt that with my experience and training, I was an above-average bodyworker. I approached the owners after more than a year of consistency, lots of compliments, an overflowing client base, and hard work.

It seemed that a year's time at this establishment had made me a senior practitioner, for many had left since I had been hired. I wanted to make a difference in this turnover. My desire was to help train practitioners and become a greater force in the business. My request was denied.

Believing that my employers would not help me reach my goals, I began seeing my own clients. I began meeting people and talking about massage. Soon, I became a wanted commodity outside of their business by doing house calls. The owners of the establishment saw this as a conflict of interest. In my mind, I was waiting for them to see I was a good businessperson and talented practitioner. I was saddened that my efforts were looked upon as conflicts. I was certain that I never broke my agreement with them, and that the fruits of my efforts were my own.

I was happy working with my employers but wanted to do more, and I was seemingly not a part of their greater plan. I was making adequate money, but I needed to pick up my own clients on the side to reach my income goals.

After my employers' declaration that I was acting in a conflicting manner, I decided to leave their business. They were not going to support my talents and simply wanted me to massage twenty people a week so they could reach their goals. I scheduled a meeting with the two owners and let them know that I felt I could not grow in their business. I told them I would uphold the contract, which stated that I was able to pay for clients at my departure. I carefully thought out my decision and requested that three clients come with me.

We agreed to the terms, and they asked me to work for two more weeks. During this time, I told no one I was leaving, upon the business owners' request, except the three clients. I didn't give my new business card to any of the other clients, realizing that how I behaved during this departure would set the tone for my new practice.

On my last day, I gave my employers a check for $1,200, or $400 per client, and left their business. I was terrified that I would not find enough clients—but not so afraid that I would break my agreement. I even saw a client at a local store who approached me and asked where I was now working. I let her know I was under contract and could not see her.

At the same time I left the business, another practitioner did, too. However, she took a pile of client information with her and had no agreement with the owners. She saw people from their business with no remorse. Two months later, she was in a car accident that left her unable to practice massage. I believe I created good karma for myself and my business through my respect for others. I hope you will choose to do the same.

If you are entering a business with a contract, act with integrity. And if you own a massage business and a new employee hesitates to sign a contract, you should question their motives. The contract should clearly state your boundaries; then it is up to the individual signing to follow.

CLIENT INFORMATION FORMS (EXAMPLE IN APPENDIX)

It is equally important to have a client information form to collect information about the current health of your clients. This is also a means of protecting yourself if you ever need to use your liability insurance. Insurance companies cannot back you unless you can show them a consent form signed by the client. Again, it is important for all practitioners to look into liability insurance and make sure you are covered. You can go online for more information about joining one of these groups. I have been a member of ABMP for ten years. If used properly, this form will provide insights that will direct the flow of your work. It can be a gateway to building a firm foundation with your clients. I always sit down with my client after the form is filled out. I am very interested in everything it says. I make sure I let the client know that the time they took to fill out the form is important to me and our session.

I begin the positive flow of energy by guaranteeing that my clients will feel relief from any aliment within an hour. Remember, a hour of massage will help any client. I give them positive feedback on what they have shared. I make suggestions and give clients options on how to approach the session, but ultimately, I leave it up to the client. I also make sure everything on the form is written clearly, especially the telephone number and address, so I am able to contact them later. I go over all of their concerns and give them the best massage of their lives.

The client information form will also help you determine whether the client has any contraindications and whether caution needs to be taken in certain areas. I keep a list of contraindications at the office, and I will not work on someone if they fit into any of those categories until I have a doctor's note in hand. I suggest, in these cases, that you do not merely accept a verbal okay. Remember, documentation is very important and will save you time and energy in the long run.

The client information form is probably the most important piece of paper in your practice. It is a gold mine of critical information. It is important to have a client's home address, home telephone, work telephone, cell phone number, and e-mail address. I use this information moments after the client leaves. I write a welcome card after the session, because clients love the consideration and thoughtfulness.

The client information form will also help you to build your client list and do consistent promotions. It is also a great tool for beginning to understand the client's needs. It is useful for finding out where the client is feeling tension and would like you to work during your session. Our client form at Freedom Massage has a picture of a human body where the client can mark pain areas. Not every client will know the names of muscles, and it is important that they are able to show you general areas.

This will also give the clients the opportunity to make note of parts of the body they do not want worked on. For instance, many folks do not want their buttocks or abs worked on during sessions. They check the box, and, without embarrassment, they are able to tell you what they do not want. It is a wonderful beginning to what could turn out to be a long-lasting relationship.

CLIENT AGREEMENT FORM (EXAMPLE IN APPENDIX)

I give clients an agreement form on their first visit that explains the house rules. It is similar to the employee contract, and it clearly states how our clients can help Freedom Massage run smoothly for mutual benefit.

One rule is that clients will be given one opportunity to miss an appointment without calling ahead twenty four hours to cancel, but then they will pay for the next appointment missed without twenty four hours notice. Another part of the agreement states, they are responsible for giving me all of the information necessary to give them a massage that will help them reach optimal health. They are responsible for giving me updates on their condition.

Through years of experience, I've gathered information and now try to stop problems before they happen. If a client misses two appointments with less then twenty four hours notice, you can present the paperwork they agreed to and signed, so that you can request payment. The agreement form is important for expressing your boundaries to the client.

The more up-front you are with your clients about the way your practice is managed, the less confusion and discussion is necessary when issues arise, and the more energy you will have to focus on bodywork. Whether you are creating your own business or working for someone else, an agreement form is especially important when managing a full appointment book. Figure out what your boundaries are, and set them by giving clients an agreement form.

CLIENT RECORDS

Take SOAP notes, or subjective, objective, assessment, and planning sheets, or client record sheets, on each client for every visit. These can be short notes describing what you did in each session. Clients love when you remember what you talked about during your last session. They feel taken care of when you can recap their concerns. It also helps you to remember areas of focus and the results.

Keeping client records will help you become closer with clients, and they will feel genuine care and interest on your part. Remember what your clients say and how they feel. Point out the progress you have made as a team. It will encourage them to come back and keep making changes in their lives, because you are making a positive difference in their lives.

I had a client who had a bad toe. During our session, he asked me to stay away from that area. I went on to give him a wonderful massage and completely avoided the area around his toe, as he requested. At our appointment the following week, I immediately asked how his toe felt, and his face lit up. He responded by saying how impressed he was that I remembered, because I had seen so many people since our last session.

It is those types of things that will make you stand out from your competition and demonstrate true professionalism. These qualities of authenticity and integrity make a true preventive care professional. We live in a society where intimate care and concern have become almost obsolete. We have the opportunity to make preventive care personal and to help people attain peace of mind. Create a form you believe will support your strengths and help you keep the best records possible.

FOLLOW-UP SHEET (EXAMPLE IN APPENDIX)

After you see a client for the first time, it is important to follow up even if they don't reschedule. Check in and see whether they still feel the wonderful effects of your work. A follow-up sheet will help you remember who you called and when.

The follow-up sheet can also be used for more long-term purposes, such as a means to get more clients in slow times. A client with the most potential for scheduling is someone who has already received a massage. The follow-up sheet is a simple way to have all your clients on a list and see the exact date you saw or contacted them last.

Don't lose track of people who have been to your practice and have not rescheduled. More importantly, do not lose track of people who were coming consistently and stopped coming. Call and let them know you when have cancellations in slow times to get them back in. Make it personal, and contact people who desire healthy living.

With the follow-up sheet, I also send out "Long Time, No See" cards to clients who have not been in for a massage in a while. The follow-up sheet is a good way to keep track of when you last sent this kind of postcard. You can order cards or write your own. My resource is the Medical Arts Press, which caters to massage practitioners and chiropractors. There are plenty of other organizations online to purchase such items. When MIA clients receive our postcards, they will often say, "I was thinking of calling, but I have not had a chance. Thanks for the reminder."

Sometimes I will even call missing clients, depending on the situation and our relationship. I just let them know that even though I have not seen them, I hope they are well, and that they are in my thoughts. Always remember, your easiest appointments to book will be with clients with whom you already have an established relationship.

Massage is an intimate business, and I feel reaching out has helped me establish nurturing qualities. It has made me aware of the pain and joys we all share as people. Remember, your client could be going through a hardship, and it might be nice for them to hear from you!

A great place to put your handy follow-up sheet is in a single follow-up folder, instead of keeping them in each client's folder. Over time, you will have too many client folders to go through to track all of your clients. I found a quick-reference folder is the easiest.

CANCELLATION SHEET (EXAMPLE IN APPENDIX)

It is great to have records, especially in slow times. The mind is incredible, but sometimes a piece of paper and a pencil are great tools for helping us recall the past. So I keep a cancellation sheet. On this form, I write down when a client cancels, and then I put it in a general cancellation folder.

This helps practitioners keep track of giving follow-up calls after cancellations. Sometimes if life is hectic and someone cancels, it is nice to call a client day or two later and have them reschedule. If the cancellation is due to a tragedy, you might send a condolence card to the client. Also, if business is slow, you can look over the cancellation list for new clients. If a client on the list never made it to your practice, you can call them and offer a discount for trying your services. A new client is an opportunity waiting to happen, because it is a potential weekly client who almost made it to the door. They are obviously interested in massage, so follow up with them.

Cancellation forms are great for both independent practitioners and businesses. Again, when you schedule new clients, get as much information as possible (name, phone number, e-mail address), so if the client cancels, you can use your cancellation form and make sure no client is overlooked. In slow times it can be used to gain clients and to assure a rescheduling possibility.

CORPORATE CHAIR MASSAGE CONTRACT (EXAMPLE IN APPENDIX)

Throughout my massage career, I have used what I've learned through repeated incidents to create forms and contracts that can help prevent problems before they occur. This form was created because I would set aside time for corporate chair massages, and clients would cancel at the last minute. These cancellations prompted one of my assistants to create a corporate chair massage contract.

We collect half the monies due for corporate chair massage when the appointment is made, when we also have them sign our contract. This ensures we will receive some, if not all, of the money we deserve for planning the event and having the practitioner ready to. It also gives validity to our agreement. It states the date we will arrive, what we need, what we will bring, and how many practitioners they requested. Previously, I had set aside time for practitioners to go out to a business and had been met by last-minute cancellations. I was left with a practitioner without work and missed potential appointments at the office because the practitioner was scheduled to go somewhere else. A potential weekly client could have been lost, because I seemingly had no coverage with the practitioner scheduled to go out on a call. I also experienced a business changing their mind last minute on the number of practitioners scheduled, because not enough people signed up for massage. I also found this to be detrimental to my business. Another reason I have a contract and want businesses to carefully consider the agreement and make a commitment to what exactly they want from my business. With a contract my practitioners and I are guaranteed a partial payment for the time we set aside and the dedication to the event. I believe a contract helps clients understand that my business is as valid as their business. Also, it gives a clear description of our services and what the client can expect—and what my employees and I expect from the client. It adds a professional edge to the service and has prevented the loss of time and money for entire afternoons when a corporate client cancels.

EMPLOYEE HANDBOOK

I give all of my employees a small handbook. It explains everything from opening to closing my facility. It clearly states my expectations of everything from attire to appreciated attitude. I suggest that if you have a business, then you provide employees with standards written in black and white.

Also, after you give them a copy, have them sign a form stating that they agree to your terms and have received a handbook. Furthermore, if you have employee interactions regarding breaking these policies, make sure you have a written note of the discussion, date it, have both parties sign, and have a witness. Documentation is crucial for protecting yourself from future troubles. Trust me, everything should be documented.

EMPLOYMENT APPLICATION (EXAMPLE IN APPENDIX)

If you have a business, a solid employment application is important. Make sure you ask the questions you feel are important for you practice, and always ask for references. Furthermore, check the references that the potential employee writes on the application.

GIFT CERTIFICATE FORM

I started my business without the gift certificate form, but as I sold more and more certificates, the process seemed to get complicated. I had an experience where a client told me they received a certificate for one massage, but they left it at home. I accepted the certificate as payment although it was not presented at the massage. Later the same client came in with the gift certificate and wanted to use it for another massage. I was put in an uncomfortable position. Did the client simply forget? Did I make a mistake? Did they pay me at the last for the last session? Without records, I was left scratching my head.

Each certificate should be given a number and an expiration date. This experience also made me realize I needed to also put notations on the certificates. On each certificate I state, "Not responsible for lost or stolen certificate. No cash refunds. Must provide certificate prior to massage." Again, I chose these three statements through experience; it is good to be up-front in managing your business.

If a client does not bring their certificate, they know in advance that they will need to pay for this session and use the certificate for the next. I do not accept a certificate as payment if there is not a certificate presented. The gift certificate form keeps track of when the certificate was sold, the amount paid, and when it was used. I try to gather as much contact information as possible upon the sale of the certificate. When the gift certificate is used, I put a check with the date indicating that the deal is done. It also helps me see how many certificates are actually used and how many have yet to come in.

In my records for bookkeeping, I do the gift certificate entry on a separate page to keep things clear. Each month, I deposit the money from the certificates. I staple the receipt from the deposit to the gift certificate form. I then staple both to the accounting record and then file it away.

PRACTITIONER RECORDS FOR PAYMENT FOR EMPLOYEES (EXAMPLE IN APPENDIX)

As an employer of massage practitioners, I think this form is ideal. Each week my practitioners collect all the monies from their massages. At week's end, we settle up. I take the money and deposit it into the Freedom Massage account, and they receive their pay via direct deposit. My employees get paid every two weeks.

One of my practitioners designed the form and decided that weeks one and two should be two different colors. At my office, week one is the white practitioner sheet, and week two is a yellow sheet. Each practitioner carefully writes down each client, the length of the session, how they were paid, and all payment and tips. At the bottom of the sheet, they transfer totals from week one to week two, making it very easy for me to do totals and pay them accordingly.

For my bookkeeping, I write down all the clients seen for the week in my accounting book, staple the receipt from the deposit to the list of clients, and then file it away. This system makes it easy to enter the clients in QuickBooks and keep records up to date.

REFERRAL TRACKING SHEET (EXAMPLE IN APPENDIX)

I like to know where my business is coming from. I have a "referred by whom" question on my client information form. I keep track of where new clients come from as a means of knowing what advertising is working and what is not. Word of mouth is still my greatest gift, and if you run a business with integrity, it will be yours too. It is important to make sure your money is well spent and to find out what works.

REQUEST TIME OFF (EXAMPLE IN APPENDIX)

My practitioners fill out this form and submit it to me to request time off. When it is approved, they write "off" with their name in the side column of our scheduling book. They also put a star next to it so everyone knows it was approved and is definite. One too many times, I was unaware when people would not be working, so to be more efficient, we use a form. Depending on your setup, things may be different, but remember that documentation is important. If you are working for an employer who does not have a form, I suggest that you write your time-off request down and have your employer acknowledge your request by signing it.

My form is simple and gives practitioners a place to list the dates they want off. It also gives them the option to request a permanent change or a temporary change. It help me plan ahead for scheduling practitioners to cover the hours and keeps the business running smoothly. We also have a file to keep the forms as a way to make sure there is no confusion in the future. Documentation is very helpful and will keep you more organized.

Conclusion

Touch is an integral part of the human experience. As an ancient art, massage has proven its healing power over the centuries. In today's hectic world, massage is increasingly needed as a means to slow down our day-to-day activities and lead people toward self-healing. Massage practitioners often enter the business in an effort to escape the corporate world, but they too often fail to consider that it is a business as well.

Through professional practice and close attention to personal energies, massage can be a viable and fruitful career, both financially and spiritually. It takes time and effort to succeed in any business that demands your body's health to keep you going. Set your goals high—but remember that it takes more than a single person to change the world through holistic care, and don't push yourself beyond your body's abilities.

It is also your clients' responsibility to respect your time and effort, and to inform you of their objectives for receiving massage. Hold them to their commitment to heal themselves with your help. In turn, it is your responsibility to grow as an effective healer. Use your voice wisely: communicate your needs within the sharing of energies, remind your clients of their potential to feel better, and help them identify the progress that they are making over time.

I would like for you to use this book to your greatest advantage. Let it be a resource in your daily experiences so that, for years to come, you can effectively aid those who need the healthful touch of your strong hands. Ensure that your life away from the massage table—our office—is as rewarding as your job. This book can serve as a reminder that sustaining your body and learning to trust your own instincts and intuition are among the keys to your success. Allow yourself to mature over time, improving your professional image, client base, and comfort while weathering the seasons of fluctuations in scheduling.

Most of all, keep this book handy to remind you of the importance of your work. Take what you have learned here and share it with others. Taking the help offered by seasoned professionals in this business will help you avoid pitfalls in your career. I gladly attribute my success to the input I've received from many mentors.

Increased interaction among professionals in preventive care fulfills a community-wide need to improve the learning curve of excellence that we are working to maintain. Don't hold back; share your gifts with others, and strive to make a difference in the daily lives of the practitioners around you, as well as the clients who trust your healing touch.

Epilogue

I am not asking you to agree with everything I have written. I just hope it helps you. There are many facets to being a massage practitioner. Your character and understanding of bodywork will deepen every day that you practice the art. If you remain positive and see it as an art, massage can be a rewarding career. The key is to believe in yourself and have fun.

I am now one of the leading providers of massage on the Main Line in Paoli, Pennsylvania. It has taken a lot of time and persistence to get where I am today in the community of bodywork. I love my work and have found it to be invigorating and thought-provoking. I have found much joy in the workings of my business, and it has taught me more about myself and other people than I ever imagined. I believe it is my genuine desire to understand the human body and mind that has pushed me to excel in my art.

I find my work rewarding, and I aspire to remain enthusiastic about learning about myself and my clients. I have realized that my work has unlimited potential and brings countless thought-provoking situations into my life. It is my goal and desire to share and learn from other bodyworkers about different concepts of massage. We all have something to teach and to learn in the massage business. I hope the art of massage will be increasingly recognized for the gift it is, through the efforts of bodywork professionals around the world.

Afterword

Diane will be appearing nationally to teach massage and bodywork professionals more about developing their careers. She will be offering additional personal stories, demonstrating massage techniques the "Freedom Way," and introducing tools to ensure the financial success of your practice. Diane will offer classes to larger audiences and also offers individualized guidance.

Interested in contacting Diane? Go to www.freedommassage.com for more information or for mentoring assistance.

APPENDIX

Form Examples

FREEDOM MASSAGE EMPLOYEE CONTRACT: SECTION ONE

I, _____, Freedom Massage therapist and bodyworker, will hereby adhere to a code of ethics and honor during my employment with Freedom Massage. I will honor any and all entities associated with Freedom Massage such as past, present, and future clients, client files and information, property, fellow therapists/bodyworkers, etc. My actions will be respectful and filled will integrity when dealing with anything regarding Freedom Massage. I will exhibit a high level of professionalism at all times, especially in the presence of clients. I will not perform any sexual misconduct during a massage/bodywork session. I will communicate openly and honestly with other members of the staff. I will demonstrate a positive attitude with regard to building my strengths as a bodyworker, as a professional and as a person.

Under no circumstances are client folders to leave the business premises. If a practitioner does not abide by this request, an immediate termination will result. I, _____, understand all clients met through Freedom Massage are not to be contacted outside of Freedom Massage. Under no circumstance, unless discussed with the owner, should a Freedom Massage client be given personal information about a practitioner (phone number, address, etc.). All interactions with Freedom Massage clients should only be done on the premises of the business. Upon termination or departure under no circumstance should practitioner _____ or anyone on practitioner's behalf contact any clients obtained through the advertising or referral network of Freedom Massage. To further denote any questions, I, _____, the practitioner will distinguish all Freedom Massage clients and/or Personal Clients on weekly Pay Sheet Form. The form will be a weekly agreement stating I clearly understand which clients belong to Freedom Massage. I, _____, understand clients who write checks directly to Freedom Massage are Freedom Massage clients. Personal Clients should be noted on the check memo, or other arrangements should be made with the owner. I, _____, the practitioner, agree there will be no exceptions.

If a practitioner would like to purchase clients, to cover advertising expenses and other expenses paid by the owner, a meeting should be arranged with the owner, prior to or after the practitioner's last day. If this system is not honored and a practitioner contacts clients, another source contacts clients on the practitioner's behalf, or the client contacts the practitioner and massages occur, the employee contract will have been broken. Therefore, there will be a penalty for every client contacted without arrangements with the owner. I, _____, the practitioner, will agree to pay a fee of $1,000.00 per client for breaking the terms of this agreement.

I, _____, the practitioner, fully understand this agreement and will not contact or massage clients outside the premises of Freedom Massage without the written consent of the owner.

Practitioners who are given a key to the building should under no circumstance use the key to enter the building outside office hours without permission from the owner. If a practitioner chooses to enter the building outside of normal business hours without contacting the owner, termination may be the result. I, _____, understand my key to Freedom Massage is to only be used during my working hours unless I contact the owner.

Freedom Massage property is to remain in the building unless special permission is given by business owner.

____ I agree to arrive 15 minutes before each session.

____ I choose to provide my own sheets and get paid a higher rate. I will use sanitary sheets for each client.

____ I decline the higher rate and wish for Freedom Massage to provide sheets.

Practitioner signature: _____
Date: _____

Witness signature: _____
Date: _____

Manager signature: _____
Date: _____

CLIENT INFORMATION FORM

Name: _____

Address: _____

City: _____ State: _____ Zip code: _____

Home #: _____ Work #: _____ Cell #: _____

May we call you at home? YES/NO   at work? YES/NO   cell? YES/NO

May we leave messages for you at home? YES/NO

E-mail address: _____

How did you hear about us? _____

In case of emergency: _____ Phone #: _____

Occupation:_____

Age: _____ Date of birth: _____

Male ☐   Female ☐

Please list any other medical practitioners seen: _____

Have you ever experienced a professional massage or bodywork session? YES/NO

If yes, how recently? _____

Primary reason for this appointment: _____

If the above condition is related to an accident or injury, please describe the incident briefly and when it occurred: _____

Does the above condition interfere with your work? YES/NO   Sleep? YES/NO

Recreation? YES/NO

Are you pregnant? YES/NO

What goals are you looking to attain from your massage session?

_____

Do you exercise? YES/NO   Type of exercise? _____ How often? _____

Do you wear contact lenses? YES/NO   dentures? YES/NO

hearing aid? YES/NO

Do you have any other medical condition(s) that the therapist should be aware of prior to administering any form of massage/bodywork? YES/NO

If yes, please specify. _____

Please check the areas of your body that you grant permission to be massaged during the session:

Head/scalp	__	Back	__	Arms	__	Feet	__
Neck	__	Buttocks	__	Chest muscles	__	Hands	__
Face	__	Legs	__	Abdomen	__		

Please check any of the following conditions that you are currently experiencing or have recently experienced:

MUSCULO-SKELETAL

__ Arthritis

__ Osteoporosis

__ TMJ dysfunction

__ Sciatica

__ Herniated disc

__ Other spine problem(s)

__ Bursitis

__ Tendonitis

CIRCULATORY

__ Varicose veins

__ Blood clots

__ High blood pressure

__ Low blood pressure

__ Phlebitis

__ Arteriosclerosis

__ Aneurysm

__ Easy bruising

__ Heart Condition

__ Other

DIGESTIVE

__ Constipation

__ Ulcerated colon

__ Spastic colon

__ Abdominal pain

__ Stomach ulcer

__ Other

MISC.

__ Cold hands/feet

__ Numb hands/feet

__ Headaches

__ Migraine headaches

__ Fatigue

__ Fainting

__ Cold or Flu

__ Shortness of breath

__ Severe depression

__ Sensitivity to lotions

__ Diabetes

__ Cancer

__ Hepatitis

__ Nerve Pain

__ Recent internal bleeding

FEMALES

__ PMS

__ Menstrual Cramps

__ Current Pregnancy

__ Insomnia   __ Skin condition(s)   __ Recent sur-
                                                    gery

__ Dizziness

Please indicate, with an "X" on the drawings below, your areas of discomfort, especially areas of tension:

[Picture with an outline of the body here for clients to mark.]

I understand that the massage/bodywork I receive at Freedom Massage is provided for the basic purpose of relaxation, relief of muscular tension, and/or for increasing circulation and energy flow. If I experience any pain or discomfort during this session, I will immediately inform the practitioner so that the pressure and/or strokes may be adjusted to my level of comfort. **I, the client, fully understand that the practitioner and/or Freedom Massage will not be held liable for any pain or discomfort following the massage session.** In fact, Freedom Massage will not be held liable for **any** reason during or following the massage session. I further understand that massage or bodywork should not be construed as a substitute for medical examination, diagnosis, or treatment, and that I should see a physician, chiropractor, or other qualified medical specialist for any mental or physical ailment of which I am aware. I understand that the massage/bodywork practitioner is not qualified to perform, diagnose, prescribe, or treat any physical or mental illness, and that nothing said in the course of the session should be construed as such. Due to the fact that massage/bodywork should not be performed under certain medical conditions, I affirm that I have stated all my known medical conditions and answered all questions honestly and accurately. I agree to keep the practitioner updated as to any changes in my medical profile and understand that there shall be no liability on the practitioner's or Freedom Massage's part should I fail to do so. I understand that I must communicate openly with the practitioner. It is the client's responsibility to make sure the practitioner and Freedom Massage have all the health information necessary for a safe and successful session.

Client signature _____ Date _____
Practitioner signature _____ Date _____

Consent to Treatment of Minor: By my signature below, I allow my child or dependent to receive massage/bodywork techniques.
Signature of parent or guardian _____ Date _____

CLIENT AGREEMENT FORM

I believe this form will help everyone fully benefit from Freedom Massage. Thank you for taking the time to read and fill out the form below. I appreciate your commitment to our place of business and to yourself. Massage will enhance your state of well-being and your life. As owner of Freedom Massage, it is my commitment to provide an excellent and professional massage.

Thanks again,
Diane Matkowski, owner of Freedom Massage

Confidentiality

-The practitioner does not share information about sessions with others.

Treatment

-The practitioner discusses what is most helpful for the specific treatment; however, the client makes the final decision. The basic purpose of the treatment is relaxation and relief of muscular tension.
-The client will make the practitioner aware of areas not to treat.
-The client will update the practitioner on any changes in health conditions or medications. There shall be no liability on the practitioner if client fails to do so.
-The client understands that massage should not be construed as a substitute for medical examination.
-The client needs to communicate pain levels to the practitioner. There shall be no liability on the practitioner if the client fails to do so.
-The client will remain covered at all times, and only the area that is being worked on will be uncovered.
-No sexual intonation/behavior is tolerated.

Time

-The client will arrive punctually for the appointment.
-Client will give a 24-hour cancellation notice.
-The client will be billed $45.00 on the second time a client does not appear for an appointment and fails to give notice of cancellation. The client will be billed $45.00 and will be billed for a full session if there is a third occurrence.

-The client will be billed $45.00 for the second late cancellation call and will be billed for a full session if there is a third late cancellation call.

-If a client arrives late for an appointment, the client will be billed for a full session and will be treated for the remaining time reserved.

-If an emergency occurs for either the client or the therapist, the session may be rescheduled by mutual agreement.

-A session can be lengthened based on practitioner's schedule.

-It is the client's responsibility to specify areas of focus during the time of the session.

Payment

-When the service is rendered, payment must be in the form of **cash or check only.**

-Gift certificates are available and are paid in advance of service; certificate is to be used within 6 months.

Agreement

The practitioner and the client agree to adhere to the boundaries specified above. If for some reason the client cannot adhere to the boundaries, the practitioner will discuss a course of action that may result in a right to refuse treatment of the client.

Client signature _____ date _____

Practitioner signature _____ date _____

Practitioner Name:

Client Name/Email	Initial Visit Date	Date called or date sent postcard	Left message or spoke to?	Did they Reschedule?	Initials

Follow-Up Sheet

CLIENT NAME	CANCELLATION REASON	APPT. DATE	DATE NOTIFIED	PHONE NUMBER	FOLLOW-UP DATE
1.					
2.					
3.					
4.					
5.					
6.					
7.					
8.					
9.					
10.					
11.					
12.					
13.					
14.					
15.					
16.					
17.					
18.					

Cancellation Form

Corporate Chair Massage Profession Services Agreement

This contract between Freedom Massage, 14 Paoli Court, Paoli, PA 19301, and [client], states that Freedom Massage will provide chair massage services on [date], from [time] to [time]. Freedom Massage will provide [number of] therapists on the day of service. Payment for services can be made by cash or check. Checks should be made payable to Freedom Massage. Half of the total amount due is to be paid as a security deposit at the time of scheduling the chair massage services. The remainder of the fee is due at the time services are rendered. Client must provide 48 hours notice for cancellation. If less than 48 hours' notice is given, the security deposit will not be refunded.

Freedom Massage will:

Provide all equipment and supplies (massage chair, paper towels, antiseptic cleaner, music, etc.) necessary to perform function.
Conform to a professional dress code.
Provide proof upon request of professional liability insurance.
Maintain confidentiality of all client information.
Be entitled to keep all tips.

Client will:

Provide use of a facility and a safe and private treatment area, its utilities and its services, including therapy space, bathrooms, parking area, etc.
Agree to payment procedures listed above.
Organize an employee chair massage sign-up sheet for the hours agreed upon above and have this prepared for the therapist(s) upon arrival.

Both parties agree that any unresolved disputes about the terms or enforcement of this agreement shall be resolved through arbitration. The non-prevailing party shall be responsible for paying all arbitration costs, unless the arbitrator finds partially for both parties, in which case all parties shall each be responsible for half the costs of arbitration.

This constitutes the entire agreement between the parties and replaces any and all prior verbal or written agreements. Should any part of this agreement be considered unenforceable by a court of competent jurisdiction, the remainder of the agreement remains in force. This agreement is governed by the laws of Pennsylvania.

Freedom Massage signature _____ Date _____

Client signature _____ Date _____

Witness signature _____ Date _____

FREEDOM MASSAGE EMPLOYMENT APPLICATION

NAME: (Last, First, M.I.) _____

ADDRESS: Street _____
         City _____ State _____ Zip _____

PHONE: Home # _____
        Work # _____
        Cell # _____

E-MAIL ADDRESS: _____

PLEASE COMPLETE THE FOLLOWING QUESTIONS:

YEARS EXPERIENCE IN THE MASSAGE THERAPY/BODYWORK FIELD: _____

SPECIALIZED MODALITIES: _____
_____
_____

CERTIFICATIONS:
_____
_____

NATIONALLY CERTIFIED? (please circle) Yes or No
If yes, please list year certification was attained. _____

HOW DID YOU HEAR ABOUT US? _____

DO YOU HAVE PROFESSIONAL LIABILITY INSURANCE? Yes or No
If yes, then with whom? _____

ARE YOU A MEMBER OF ANY PROFESSIONAL ORGANIZATIONS? (please list)

_____

EDUCATION LEVEL:

Please check if completed INSTITUTION YEAR	
High school or equivalent □	
College	2-year Associate's □
	4-year Bachelor's □
Master's □	
Doctorate □	
Specialty/Vocational School □	

EMPLOYMENT HISTORY: (please list most recent company first)

Company:	Date started:
	Date ended:
Address:	
Former Manager:	Title:
Contact number:	
Reason for leaving:	

Company:	Date started:
	Date ended:
Address:	
Former Manager:	Title:
Contact number:	
Reason for leaving:	

Company:	Date started:
	Date ended:
Address:	
Former Manager:	Title:
Contact number:	
Reason for leaving:	
Company:	Date started:
	Date ended:
Address:	
Former Manager:	Title:
Reason for leaving:	
Company:	Date started:
	Date ended:
Address:	
Former Manager:	Title:
Contact number:	
Reason for leaving:	

REFERENCE LIST: (please list at least 3 professional references)

Name:	
Company:	Title:
Phone number:	
Relationship:	
Contact number:	

Name:

Company: Title:

Phone number:

Relationship:

Contact number:

Name:

Company: Title:

Phone number:

Relationship:

Contact number:

Name:

Company: Title:

Phone number:

Relationship:

Contact number:

I hereby testify that the information provided above is correct and accurate. I allow Freedom Massage to contact any former employer listed above to verify the employment dates as well as to contact the people listed above as professional references. I also authorize and allow Freedom Massage to contact me at any of the numbers I have provided above. I understand that the information I have provided to Freedom Massage will be kept private and confidential.

Applicant signature: _____ *Date:* _____

Freedom Massage signature: _____ *Date:* _____

Practitioner Records for Payment for Employees

Practitioner Record for Week Ending:								
Practitioner Name:								
	Client Name	Date		Cash Amt.	Check Amt.	Tips	G.C.#	Length (30/60/90)	Comments
1									
2									
3									
4									
5									
6									
7									
8									
9									
10									
11									
12									
13									
14									
15									
16									
17									
18									
19									
20									

				Total for Pay Period Ending:				
Week Ending								
Total Massages								
30 minute		+		=				
30 minute/personal		+		=				
60 minute		+		=				
60 minute/house calls		+		=				
60 minute/personal		+		=				
90 minute		+		=				
90 minute/house calls		+		=				
90 minute/personal		+		=				
Total Cash:	$							
Total Tips:	$	+		=				

Please be sure to total cash only and record number of massages. Love you all ...
Thanks for your efforts and hard work!

CLIENT NAME	REFERRAL SOURCE

Referral Tracking Sheet

REQUEST FOR TIME OFF/HOURS CHANGE FORM

Name: _____

Date: _____

Please list below the day(s) and/or date(s) that you would like to request time off:

_____

_____

_____

_____

Please list the day(s) and time(s) that you would like to change:

Current Day	Time Frame	Proposed Change	Temp or Perm?

Please put this on Diane's desk upon completion. Thanks. ☺

****

Office use only

Approved & Signature: _____

- Yes

- No

About the Author

Diane R. Matkowski began her business, Freedom Massage, in Paoli, Pennsylvania, almost ten years ago. Today, more than two thousand clients and a growing number of massage practitioners have shared the art of massage within its walls. Diane has enjoyed mentoring practitioners and helping them build a solid client base.

i) Your body responds
very nice to the massage

978-0-595-43477-0
0-595-43477-0

(Dr ~~Depa~~ Book) (money mind)

Expand energy   Desire
Invest in self   and
Ritual and practice   Belief
     to make money

show up plant
     seeds
celebrate and amblifly
_____

When you invest in self money
    comes back.
          Money Ritual

1) Set a farm date it
        Bank accounts. I love you
        date with it. A love note
        Dream and Dance and make love
with money Get a money tree.
2) Pic a symbol what makes you
      feel rich

I am calling in extra 2000.~~00~~
week
- I am worthy of this money to
    help myself and make others smile
3) Money Alter ~~~~ I am worthy
        and wealty because.